END BORING

(404) 458-7323
info@iphp.store

Second Edition
ISBN: 978-0-9936247-1-1 (paperback)
ISBN: 978-0-9936247-3-5 (ebook)
ISBN: 978-0-9936247-2-8 (hardcover)
ISBN: 978-0-9936247-4-2 (audiobook)

Ordering Information:
Special discounts are available on quantity purchases by corporations, associations, and others. For details, contact info@iphp.store

END BORING

A TACTICAL APPROACH TO PUBLIC SPEAKING AND COMMUNICATION

IVAN WANIS RUIZ

Special thanks to the following people who helped me with this book. This book was just an idea and a series of disjointed thoughts until I had the great fortune to meet you.

Sharada Weir

Huafeng Pei

Chris Peterson

Simone Abrahamsohn

Alejandro Telo

Lisa Casagrande

Daniel Wanis Ruiz

Lisa Finlay

Elizabeth Stetar

Kirby Rae

Samia Moussad

Cheryl Lee

Maria Teresita Santos

Ana Lucia Escobar Cifuente

Camilo Ruiz Ferro

CONTENTS

DISCLAIMER

THANK YOU FOR BUYING MY BOOK. Although you have purchased this book, it remains the copyrighted property of the author and may not be reproduced, copied, or distributed for commercial or non-commercial purposes. If you enjoy this book, please encourage your friends to download their own copy. Thank you for your support.

This guide is for informational purposes only. You should always seek out other avenues of information before acting on something that I have recommended. Understand that there are links contained in this guide that I may benefit from financially.

The material in this guide may include references to information, products, and/or services by third parties. I do not assume responsibility or liability for any third-party material or opinion. Reference to such third-party materials in this guide does not constitute my guarantee of any information, instruction, opinion, products, or services contained within the third-party material. The use of recommended third-party material does not guarantee any success.

No part of this publication shall be reproduced, transmitted, or sold in whole or in part in any form without the prior written consent of the author. All trademarks and registered trademarks appearing in this guide are the property of their respective owners.

Users of this guide are advised to exercise due diligence when it comes to making business decisions based on information contained within the guide. All information, products, and services that have been referenced should be independently verified by qualified professionals. In reading this guide, you agree that neither I nor my company is responsible for any outcome, positive or negative, resulting from decisions made based on information presented in this guide. Examples given are for informational purposes only, and their use is subject to reader discretion, with the understanding that results may vary.

EVERYONE IS WRONG

A LIFETIME OF FRUSTRATION MADE THIS BOOK

This book was born from frustration! Frustration that no one seems to be able to do what they're teaching when it comes to speaking and communication. Everyone is either trying to teach you how to be a motivational speaker or some BS on overcoming your fears. In other words, it's all self-help. But what does facing your fears and embracing your passion have to do with your regional sales report? Or a meeting with five people? Or doing a quarterly update for your company? Or a presentation in university? Nothing!

Another reason I wrote this book: from frustration with all the people that try to teach us how to be good speakers and impactful speakers while they themselves are terrible at it. How on earth are you telling me how to speak if your training session is boring? If you have ever taken a public speaking course, chances are you've been bored through most of it. Just sitting and listening most of the time. You may have heard some good ideas, but they were ideas without substance. Like quotes that sound really good but don't actually change your behavior.

Why does this keep happening? Most communication experts just decided they were communication experts. They worked in sales or marketing their whole lives—but those are specific fields—and just because someone worked in one of those fields for years doesn't mean that they are any good at public speaking. Others just have great personalities and essentially try to teach you their personality, but this is impossible. Some maybe did improv or stand-up comedy so they teach you communication from that perspective.

They probably took all their examples from their fields or their personal experiences and, as a result, those ideas are hard to translate to your situation. Again, just good ideas without substance. Things like:

- Know your audience
- Make sure to connect with your audience
- Practice, practice, practice
- Try to speak with passion
- Have a clear message

Obvious, right? If you have done any communication training, you have heard these goals. On the surface they are great ideas, but that is the problem: no one goes to the next step and shows you tactics to achieve these goals. They will tell you to do this, but not how to recognize if you are actually doing this.

So, in essence, there are three big problems with the current state of public speaking education and training:

1. None of it is practical
2. It doesn't apply to most of our day-to-day speaking needs
3. The people teaching us aren't themselves great speakers

I realize that the market is saturated with public speaking resources that all make the same promise: to make you a better public speaker. So what makes this book any different?

Real Speakers

Most "public speaking experts" are from the corporate world and have never had real-world experience outside of marketing or sales, for example. I went out and found people who actually do it in their day-to-day lives. Yes, I spoke to stand-up comics, but also buskers, ring announcers, and professional wrestlers, to name a few. These individuals have the remarkable capacity to attract audiences, bring in a crowd, spark emotions and excitement while commanding their attention.

Real Experts

I spoke to police interrogators and professional poker players. I asked them, how do you know when someone is lying? How do you know when someone is bluffing?

Real Science

I researched evolution, psychology, biology, and neuroscience to figure out how the brain functions and how it has evolved to absorb and process information.

Real Tactics

I took what I learned, and instead of giving you general ideas, this book will go a step further and literally give you physical tactics and actual sentence structures that you can use to make yourself more impactful right away.

Real Examples

Instead of a bunch of general examples or hypothetical situations, I will give you nothing but specific examples from a variety of industries and backgrounds from previous participants of my training courses.

In a perfect world, whether presenting at a training seminar, leading a meeting, or sharing something in front of a classroom, people would look forward to your presentation, and you and your audience would leave feeling excited and energized. This book can help us make this a reality.

I am on a mission to end boring and I need your help. So don't just read this book. Please try to apply it, and let's make this perfect world a reality.

BATMAN, BOWS, AND ARROWS

Public speaking has traditionally been considered a soft skill. We tend to think that you either have it or you don't…an innate talent. I'm here to challenge that idea and show you tactics that you can practice to make yourself a better public speaker.

Have you ever shot a bow and arrow? The mechanics of a bow and arrow are extremely straightforward. You can understand how it works in seconds. But do you hit a bullseye every time? No. To become extremely proficient at this simple task, it requires lots and lots of repetition and physical practice.

I believe that being charismatic, engaging, and a great speaker is a series of physical actions that you can learn and practice. In the same way that you can learn to be really good with the bow and arrow by physically practicing, so can you learn to be an awesome speaker by physically practicing the things that I'm about to show you.

Public speaking has always lain in the realm of soft skills. We tend to think that you either have it or you don't…that you're born with it. Certainly, there are people who might seem like naturals, but guaranteed they learned it. I'm here to challenge the idea that speaking is a soft skill and show you concrete tactics that you can practice to make yourself a better public speaker.

Here is another key idea you need to understand: there is no right way. The way I speak is not the way you speak. My personality is not your personality. Therefore, in this book, I am not teaching you rules, I'm teaching you tools. Instead of giving you some random advice based on my personality, which you cannot use, I want you to become Batman. Batman has a utility belt of tools that he can use in a variety of situations. Are they all needed all the time? No! But that doesn't matter—the important part is that for every situation, you will have a variety of tools that you can use to make your communication better in that situation.

THE FUTURE IS NOT ONLINE

Everyone has been saying for years that the future of work, the future of business, is going to be online. This is not fully true. We've been working online for a long time. I'm going to say this again in the last chapter, but I want to say it here as well: ***The future is not online, the future is -LIVE- online.***

As much as we have talked about virtual work and working from home, the need to speak to each other will always be there. The only difference in the years to come is that some—not all—of this communication will happen over a laptop.

I dedicated the last chapter of this book to communication strategies specifically for virtual communication. Batman is all about embracing technology and so should we. Your tool belt will not be complete unless you can apply it and use tactics for live virtual communication. I want you to stand out the next time you have a virtual meeting, a virtual presentation, and/or are teaching online. That's why the last chapter of this book will give you even more tools that you can apply specifically the next time you're on Zoom, Microsoft Teams or Webex or whatever online platform you use.

DON'T READ, SCAN

I wrote this book as a reference, not as something to read from beginning to end. I mean, if you're really interested in it, please do read it from front to back, but more importantly, keep it with you and use it the next time you have to make a speech or presentation. This book is all about tools. So, for example, when you need to think of how to do an opening, you can refer to the Openings section in chapter 2. When you're not sure how to transition between topics, look at the Transitions section.

I did this on purpose, and this is crucial and something you really need to understand. Unless you try to apply the strategies, this book is just an interesting read from a very opinionated trainer. Learn by trying and doing, and just like with a bow and arrow, the more you try these tactics the better you'll become at public speaking and communication.

Are you ready?

ARE YOU A LIAR?

IN THIS CHAPTER WE WILL INTRODUCE two fundamental concepts that will completely change your perspective on communication: first, what people actually remember, and second, the surprising similarities between public speaking and lying.

THE TRUTH WILL SET YOU FREE, BUT FIRST IT WILL PISS YOU OFF.

– Gloria Steinem

THE 2% RULE

Have you ever tried to repeat a joke you heard a stand-up comic say? How well did you do? Chances are you ruined it. And it probably went something like this…

"I heard this really funny joke…I can't really remember how it goes, but it was super funny, and you should check it out, and there's this whole part about closing the door…but it's really funny when they do it!"

Does that sound familiar? The reason it never works when you try to repeat a joke is because of what you remember. Think about your own experience when you hear something really funny and you try to repeat it to someone. Your recall is usually a general impression. "I saw this really funny thing. You have to check it out. It was really funny…" and probably one thing they said, like "close the door." That's it. That's all you remember. And let's face it, that's comedy. That's something you want to remember. It's not work and it's not school. This is the first concept that you need to get in your head. It's not about what you say. It's about what people remember.

The underlying principle that applies to every tactic and idea in this book is the 2% rule. You probably think that if you give a good presentation, the audience will remember what you were trying to tell them. But no matter how good the speaker is, most people will only retain about 2% of a presentation. Afterwards, most people will really only remember:

- One piece of information (e.g., a fact or number)
- A general impression of you (the speaker)

The smart speaker decides what these will be in advance and repeatedly emphasizes them.

What Is the Goal?

If you have ever had communication or public speaking training, you have heard that the goal of a presentation is something like this:

- To inform
- To persuade
- To get the audience to act on something
- To convince them of something

But what are the odds that you will actually achieve this? What are the odds that everyone will remember everything, everyone will be convinced, everyone will be persuaded? Probably very low, if not zero. Therefore, if you think about it, everything we have been told is a "goal" for a presentation doesn't work. It's setting yourself up for failure! Here is the worst part: you know it doesn't work, yet you still do it! Why? Because no one has given us an alternative…until now.

The trap so many of us fall into when we speak is information overload—we go into too much detail. We think that the more we give, the clearer it will be, but that is not the case. Good speeches and good presentations don't tell you everything you need to know. They make you want to know more. In other words: **The goal of a presentation is to create curiosity.**

If you can make someone curious, then they will do the work for you! If you can make them curious, they will want to find out more on their own. They will actually read the slides or the materials you leave behind. They will spend their time thinking about your ideas. If they are curious, they will invest time to find out more.

Want a sign of a successful speech? When you are done, there is a line of people waiting to talk to you afterward.

How do we achieve this? How do we create curiosity? That is what you are about to learn.

THE LIAR'S PARALLEL

When I was researching communication, I decided to only approach and study people who do it for real in their day-to-day lives, not people who teach it. My first two stops were with a police interrogator and a professional poker player. I wanted to know what to look for to see whether or not someone is telling the truth. I wanted to know how to tell if someone is bluffing.

What I found out was shocking. The way people speak when they are presenting or speaking in front of others is the same way people speak when they are lying! You see, in both situations people are scared and nervous. These feelings bring about similar physiological changes, and as a result, the liar and the nervous speaker communicate in the same way.

People who are speaking in front of others and people who are lying fall into three general traps. I call this **The Liar's Parallel**:

1. Formal language
2. Distance
3. Too many details

Formal Language

Have you ever sent a text message/SMS? Of course, we all have. Have you noticed that they barely resemble language anymore? It's symbols, weird abbreviations, codes, etc. Yet we can all understand them. Why? Because a text message is not written language, it's our attempt to replicate verbal language, and the way we write is not the way we speak.

This idea is further explained by John McWhorter, an associate professor of English and comparative literature at Columbia University. He has written several books on language. One of my favorites is *Words on the Move: Why English Won't – and Can't – Sit Still (Like, Literally)*.

Check out the QR link or go to publicspeakinglab.com/verbal to see John explain this idea further.

We know that the way you write is not the way you speak, and if you write your presentation out word for word, you will fall into this trap, guaranteed. You can always tell when someone has memorized something because it tends to sound a little weird. This is also true when someone is trying to be "professional." You can always tell! It's because they are using words they wouldn't use in a normal conversation. I call it "businessese." When someone speaks this way, you start tuning it out because it's not natural and sounds insincere. As a result, it is also very hard to retain any information.

Now, I'm not saying that you should be super casual with your superiors or your professors or whomever you are speaking in front of. What I am saying is that there's a difference between speaking like you are reading from an essay and speaking like a normal person. Let's look at some examples:

LESS EFFECTIVE	MORE EFFECTIVE
My goal is to identify the key factors I can utilize, sharpening and effectively using my skills in a competitive environment and helping to accomplish business goals. Growing as a student and growing along with the institution that I choose to be a part of occupy important slots in my list of priorities.	I really want a job that can teach me to be a better analyst and where I could expect to get a promotion within a few years if I do a good job.
To entertain, inform, and inspire people around the globe through the power of unparalleled storytelling, reflecting the iconic brands, creative minds, and innovative technologies that make ours the world's premier entertainment company.	We use everything, from movies to theme parks to toys and television, to make our brand one of the most recognized in the world.
To empower and educate people everywhere so that they can improve their lives and achieve their goals.	To run virtual seminars on Zoom and give people a formula to say why they are awesome without bragging.

Distance

Here is an unpleasant truth. Anecdotes are not evidence, but they are more convincing than evidence. One personal experience will do more to convince someone than 10 peer-reviewed papers. It's why someone watches one YouTube video and then believes some weird food is healthy or that the pyramids were created by aliens. It's not right, but it is how the brain works.

Speaking in "you," "we," and "they" are different sub-problems of a failure to use first-person language. You see the "we" language is not something we can picture. It is not something we can act upon and it comes across like you are trying to tell everyone what to do.

I know what you are thinking, "What's wrong with that?" Isn't that what we are trying to do when we are speaking in front of others? There is another factor at play there, and it's something psychologists call psychological reactance (PR).

What is PR? Well, let me ask you something. Have your parents ever told you what to do? How to live your life? Now let me ask you another question. How often do you ignore their advice? How often do you ignore their advice even though you know they are right?

When I was 15 years old, I remember going out one night. I was reaching for my jacket when I heard my mother telling me to wear a jacket. Even though I was planning on wearing a jacket, the second she told me to do it, I had this urge to say no. Even though it was cold, I ended up leaving without the jacket. Even though it made sense, even though she was right, even though it's what I wanted, I still didn't do it! Why? Because I didn't like being told what to do. Which is something, dear reader, I think we have in common. In fact, I can tell you that it's something almost every human being in this world has in common. That is psychological reactance. It is when you do the opposite or resist what someone is saying because you feel like they are infringing on your freedom to choose. This is not something that I made up, by the way. This is straight from the psychology literature. You can look it up for yourself.

Here is a quick video explaining reactance further: publicspeakinglab.com/reactance

Why am I telling you this? When you speak in the second person, this is typically what you are doing: telling people what to do. When you use terms like "you should," or "it's important that you," or "you need to prepare," the reflexive response is to resist the idea and not want to do it. It's not that people are stubborn; it's that we feel like our freedom to choose has been threatened, and as such, we resist it in order to assert control in our decision-making. When I want to be persuasive, I don't tell the audience what they should do! (See what I did there?)

LESS EFFECTIVE	MORE EFFECTIVE
You should make your first slide something that sets the tone and engages your audience.	I always start my presentation with a high-definition picture that at first seems unrelated to my topic.

Using "we" is essentially the same thing as "you" because that is just a polite way of telling people what to do.

Now that we have covered you and we…what's wrong with "they" (in other words, speaking in third person)? When we use distancing language, it has a sense of insincerity to it. It sounds like something we should be reading, not something we are saying. If speaking in third person actually worked, then everyone who has ever listened to a self-help guru would have all of their problems solved. Let me try it on you, and you tell me how well it works.

> "It is important to focus on the positive aspects of life. People should value themselves and what they do. Making the world a better place is a goal that everyone needs to consider when thinking about their lives…"

Have you stopped rolling your eyes yet? ;) It's not that it's wrong, but rather so general that it means nothing. Good ideas become cliché when we speak in third person.

This is why it's so powerful to speak in "I" statements. Speaking in first person is how truly persuasive people communicate. Let me prove it to you. Have you ever watched a promo video for some new workout? If you've ever watched these fitness infomercials, you know exactly what I'm talking about. They spend the vast majority of the time showing you "before and after" pictures and highlighting personal experiences. Even though there's a disclaimer underneath saying that these are not typical results, even though you know it's overstating the results, it still manages to get your attention, and it still manages to make you think.

LESS EFFECTIVE	MORE EFFECTIVE
It is important that people make good financial investments and consider all their options when considering what instruments to take advantage of.	When I wanted to invest in the stock market, I first learned the difference between stocks, bonds, mutual funds, ETFs, and futures.
Buyers have to do rigorous analyses of demographic data before making real estate decisions.	I never buy a house without looking at how many new people will be living in the area in five years. If it is above 5% growth, I know there is an opportunity.

Question: What happens if you use "we" when explaining? Does that also count as falling into this trap? Yes, since it goes back to telling people what to do.

I know what you are thinking. Sometimes you have to use "we" or "they" because it's the most appropriate way to explain or recommend something. Or maybe you feel like too many "I" statements will seem unprofessional. Or in your industry speaking formally is what people want. Or even worse…What if I am wrong???

Certainly, I am trying to convince you otherwise, but suppose you are right. What do you do then? Well, this book will provide lots of strategies, but here is a little preview: **Do both!** Start how you normally might but follow up with an anecdote or a specific example. This way you lose nothing, and still enhance your message.

Explain something with a "we" or "they," then follow up with a personal anecdote. Let's go back to the example above:

We should focus on the positive aspects of life. People should value themselves and what they do. We need to make the world a better place, that is a goal that everyone needs to consider when thinking about their lives…

[then follow this up with]

I spend five minutes every Sunday afternoon writing down the good things that happened to me that week. Every year, I post that list on my social media.

It is important for us to understand our clients' full financial position so we can better address their retirement needs.

[then follow this up with]

We managed to advance a client's retirement from 70 to 55 once they let us know what other investments they had in another bank.

Too Many Details

This is the one that I always struggle with. It's trying to say less, refrain from talking and talking and talking. Giving more information and thinking it will make your points clearer. Also not knowing when to stop. You know you're falling into this trap when:

- You repeat what is written on a slide and then expand on it. So, you're telling people stuff that they can obviously read and then using phrases like, "yeah, so basically, this is saying about…"

- Someone asks you a question and it takes you more than 30 seconds to answer it.
- You finish what you are saying and then keep on talking, repeating what you just said, until it just fizzles out.

I am not going to bore you with examples and videos of people going into too much detail because it's the majority of what you already see and hear in every presentation. Instead, let's talk about solutions. Let's talk about the Ig Nobel Prizes.

The Ig Nobel Prizes, organized and presented by the scientific humor magazine *Annals of Improbable Research*, are one of the truly wonderful events in this world. The goal is to "honor achievements that first make people LAUGH, and then make them THINK."

Why are we talking about the Ig Nobel? Because they present a solution to too many details. Part of this annual event includes the "24/7" challenge. In an attempt to make things fun, but also digestible and easy to remember, every year they have a challenge where renowned subject matter experts must:

- First, provide a complete, technical description in 24 seconds.
- Then, provide a clear summary that anyone can understand in just seven words.

The goal is not just to have fun, but also to challenge the academic thinking of what it means to effectively communicate ideas. Every time I bring up the concept of the "details trap" when I'm teaching communication, there's always a valid and understandable concern about subject matter. Inevitably, someone brings up the fact that in their subject area, they must provide details, or that it's not possible to simplify concepts for their topic, or that they are speaking to an educated audience, so they are required to include details. The Ig Nobels challenge this way of thinking by championing another viewpoint: complex ideas can always be boiled down to simple concepts. After all, was it not Albert Einstein who said, "If you can't explain it simply, you don't understand it well enough"?

Simplicity is not just something that is possible, it is something that people want. When I am challenged with the idea that people want the details or want it to be technical, I always respond with, "Is that what you want?" If you are at a conference, within your area of expertise, do you want an hour-long technical explanation or do you want someone to give you the core idea, the exciting possibilities? When was the last time you sat in a workshop or training and actively read the whole slide? The whole reason TED Talks became so popular was that they took the technical and complex and presented it in a compelling way—and remember, originally these talks were in front of experts in the subjects.

Clare Boothe Luce was a successful playwright who became one of the first female U.S. ambassadors, and she wrote "...the height of sophistication is simplicity." Which brings us back to the Ig Nobles. Before we get into the strategy, let's first look at a few examples.

You can view all these examples via the QR code or by going to publicspeakinglab.com/details.

Take a moment and ask yourself a few questions:

1. With the technical explanation, how quickly did you tune out? Five seconds? Ten?
2. Irrespective of how slow or fast they spoke in the technical explanation, how much did you really understand or absorb?
3. How often did the seven words get a reaction out of you? Make you interested?
4. Imagine if they started with the seven words? How much would that have helped you to understand the technical explanation?

With all that being said, how much detail is too much detail? Is there a rule we can apply for our next session? Well, dear reader, the truth is…I don't believe in rules, I believe in tools. There is no perfect amount of detail because that will vary based on your subject matter and the time you have. However, there is a great exercise to help you discover what the perfect amount of detail is for your situation:

- Run your presentation normally and time it
- Try the same speech, touching on all the points but in half the time
- Repeat this until you are down to two minutes
- Try the same speech, touching on all the points but in two minutes
- Try the same speech, touching on all the points but in 30 seconds
- Try the same speech, touching on all the points but in 10 seconds
- Try the same speech, touching on all the points but using the old Twitter limit (150 characters)

- Try the same speech, touching on all the points but with only 20 words.

Expressing your ideas with increasing limitations will help you identify what is the essence of your message and what is just…too many details.

While going through each step will really help you, if you have time limitations or minimal time to practice, then just use whatever time constraint is most appropriate. I have one caveat, though: always try to get it to one sentence. Even if you fail, being able to summarize or package your presentation into one clean sentence will dramatically increase retention and interest. Check out the next chapter of this book for more strategies to make impactful sentences.

Here is another variation on this strategy you can use if you have an hour or more or if you are teaching a class over several hours. You can apply this strategy for each section. For example, if you have a presentation that is an hour long and it's broken up into five sections, then you can apply this strategy to each section.

Remember, the goal of a presentation is to create curiosity. Details kill curiosity.

DON'T FORGET

- After a presentation, most people will only remember one thing you said and a general impression.
- The goal of a presentation is to create curiosity so the audience will want to find out more on their own.
- People who are lying and people who are speaking in public communicate the same way

CASE STUDY
AVOIDING REACTANCE

Rayjan is a salesman in the industrial sector.

"Selling over the phone is a little bit more difficult, since you do not see the customers' faces and how they react when you tell them about the price. For example, this Friday we had a call with a new client, and we presented five options. They told us: 'We liked the five concepts you showed us.' As a side note, we showed them the high-end version all the way down to the low cost, or as I like to say, 'cost-efficient,' version.

Long story short, the customer told us: 'We liked the high-end solution you showed us, but we want the cost-efficient price…could you work on a mid-level solution with X and Y features?'

So now we know which features are more interesting for them and which ones do not add value to their process (from their point of view), and we will work on the tailored solution to meet their needs. If we had just presented what we thought they wanted, or just the most expensive solution, we would have never gotten the insights and probably would not have gotten a new client."

CHAPTER TWO

THERE CAN BE ONLY ONE

THIS CHAPTER WILL BE FOCUSED ON the first part of the 2% rule. It's an exploration of diverse strategies engineered to etch your desired message into people's memory. Each one is a tool that can be used independently or in combination with the others.

IF YOU CAN'T WRITE YOUR MESSAGE IN A SENTENCE YOU CAN'T SAY IT IN AN HOUR.

- Dianna Booher

THE VISCERAL STATEMENT (VS)

My former business partner had a test for explanations. He would say "give it to me in a sentence," cutting off the other person if they had been talking for too long (which was usually after about a minute or so). If they couldn't, they were disregarded for not knowing their topic well enough. By packaging your presentation into a single sentence, you are generating interest and letting your audience know right away what they can expect. This concise and informative sentence acts as a guiding principle throughout your speech, reinforcing the core concept you want your audience to remember.

That is nothing new. So, here is where we can go next-level. Here is where we can create curiosity and impact. Whatever this sentence is, it has to be specific enough that someone can agree or disagree. Either result is awesome. Why? Because we are looking for reactions. The more visceral a reaction, the more likely someone will remember what caused the reaction. This is based in biology. Visceral reactions, by definition, provoke biological responses—like an increase in cortisol that leads to the release of adrenaline and changes in heart rate. This is an evolutionary survival mechanism to help us better address future situations by embedding the cause of the reaction in long-term memory.

Suppose you say your VS and someone disagrees…good! That means that they will likely be trying to find a way to tear apart your information, and it means that they are listening and reading, which means that you got them to pay attention!

Suppose that they agree with you…good! Do you know what people love being? People love being right. Which means that now they're paying attention because it's their smart idea that you're presenting.

Let's look at some examples of less and more effective visceral statements.

LESS EFFECTIVE	MORE EFFECTIVE
We need to better leverage our social media presence to engage with our customers.	Every week, we should have a random employee "hijack" our Instagram account.
Dropbox should focus its growth strategy on developing markets.	Dropbox needs to invest heavily in advertising in Brazil, Nigeria, and the UAE.
H&M needs to pivot its current competitive strategy and focus more on eastern markets and focus on marketing	By creating a "Man of the Year" campaign for the most stylish man in China, we can become top of mind for high-end fashion.

What is the real difference here? If you think about it, all of the "less effective" examples are concise and easy to remember, yet they lack specificity, which, in turn, fails to elicit a visceral response. The "more effective" ones, however, are easier to imagine and prompt agreement or disagreement. They also provoke questions like, "why?" and "how would that work?" igniting a deeper engagement and exploration of the idea.

The Visceral Statement is therefore a single sentence that highlights a very specific example that compels the listener to take some sort of action or form an opinion. If it's not specific, it's not useful.

THE GOAL OPPORTUNITY STATEMENT

Now that you've come up with your Visceral Statement, you can also choose to expand it into a Goal Opportunity Statement (GOS). Let me be clear: you don't have to do this, but it is another option depending on the information you have on hand.

Your GOS differs from the visceral statement in that it adds measurability—in other words, some sort of number you can use as a metric for success. This number can be time, money, percent, increase, decrease, volume, or anything, really, as long as it is something that you can measure. In the words of one of the greatest rappers of the 1980s, DJ Quik.

IF IT DON'T MAKE DOLLARS IT DON'T MAKE SENSE.
—TRACK DOLLAZ + SENSE

The GOS works because it gives us a number. No matter how cool, interesting, life-changing, or life-saving an idea is, remember that one of the first questions in the listener's mind is always going to be a number—how much, how long, etc. The GOS allows us to address this initial question and again primes the listener to know what to expect from the rest of the presentation.

The GOS is made up of three elements. The first is the specific visceral action that the listener can agree or disagree with. The other two elements, benefit and time, add measurability. The benefit refers to any kind of number (percent, dollar amount, quantity, customers, etc.), and the time is some unit of, well, time.

Substitute your own information into these examples or create similar statements to make them relevant to your topic.

By creating a graffiti "safe space" in the downtown core, we can decrease vandalism by 20% in one year.

By creating donuts inspired by chocolate bars, Dunkin Donuts can increase its revenue by 10% over the next five years.

Refining lignin from tree bark scraps can more than quadruple the vanilla supply within 10 years.

Letting a different employee take over our Instagram channel for the next 30 days can help us go viral before the end of the month.

I realize that sometimes we might not know or have access to numerical data. What do you do then? Well, that's where the visceral statement comes into play. Additionally, two other points merit discussion.

First, you don't necessarily need both numbers; one suffices. For instance, in the absence of financial information, time can serve as a measurable factor, and vice versa.

Second, remember that the world runs on reasonable assumptions. Don't be afraid to make a few assumptions to derive some sort of numbers. As long as you are clear that it is an assumption and can provide the information for that assumption you are safe. The world runs on reasonable assumptions because, despite our desires, predicting the future remains beyond our capability.

GOAL OPPORTUNITY QUESTION

The moment you're asked a question, there's a span of time where your mind exclusively focuses on the question and the answer. It's like a reflex. A third strategy for clearly summarizing your presentation and focusing your audience is, therefore, converting your Visceral Statement or your Goal Opportunity Statement into a question—a question that you can keep repeating throughout your presentation. This promotes continued curiosity. Let's take a look at our previous examples and see how we can convert them into questions.

Is there a way to use vandalism to benefit the city?

How can a graffiti zone actually reduce graffiti by 20%?

How can Dunkin Donuts increase its revenue by 10% while competing with Starbucks and Tim Hortons?

Is there a way to cheaply make vanilla?

What would happen if we let our employees take over our Instagram?

Notice that all these statements beg a question and allude to a direction for your presentation via an answer, so that right away everyone will know what you are going to talk about and what information they should walk away with. You've also primed your audience to anticipate an answer to this question. The effect parallels a TV show's technique of leaving you with a cliffhanger or a 'To Be Continued' ending—now you're compelled to watch the next episode, or in our scenario, to keep listening to the presentation.

THE KNOW-PHRASE

A question presents itself: How can you repeat your GOS or your VS without sounding like you are repeating yourself all the time? This brings us to our fourth option of summarization: using a Know-Phrase!

A Know-Phrase is essentially just a repackaging of the specific information in your GOS/VS into a fun and "catchy" form. Think about it as the billboard version of your presentation. It is not meant to give information but to help the listener remember information by putting an easy to remember phrase in their mind.

The beauty of this approach is that it provides the listener with a schema (mental shortcut) that helps the listener to recall more information from your presentation. It also helps to summarize the general idea of what you said but in a more novel way.

Consider the following examples:

- Barack Obama's "Yes, We Can"
- Nike's "Just Do It!"
- Airbnb's "Belong Anywhere"
- Disneyland's "The Happiest Place on Earth"

Another way to think about it is creating unique idioms. An idiom is a phrase that doesn't mean exactly what the words say. Instead, it has a special meaning understood by a group of people.

- "Piece of cake" - When something is very easy.
- "Break a leg" - To wish someone good luck.

- "Costs an arm and a leg" - Something is very expensive.
- "Hit the hay" - To go to bed and sleep.
- "Bite the bullet" - Facing a difficult situation or enduring something unpleasant.

If you are an English speaker, I don't have to tell you where these phrases come from. Not only do you know them, you probably have certain images, opinions, and values associated with them. This makes them not only relevant on a personal level but also memorable.

In each of the idioms above, you can see that the phrase itself conjures lots of information; it acts as an anchor that makes you think of deeper meaning. What would happen if we created a unique idiom for our presentation?

Yet a third strategy to create a Know-Phrase is to associate your idea or the thesis of your presentation with something that people already know. It can be a brand, an app, a service, etc. that is ubiquitous. Or in other words, creating a simile. A simile is a figure of speech that compares two things by using the words "like'" or "as" to highlight a particular similarity between them. It's a way of expressing a similarity between two different objects or ideas to create a vivid or descriptive image. The most used format is saying something is "like the X of Y" to emphasize a particular quality, characteristic, or similarity between the two entities. For example, when you say your idea, service or product is like:

- The AirBnb of [___]
- The Ferrari of
- The Michael Jordan of
- The Netflix of

Let's once again go back to our previous VS and GOS and craft some Know-Phrases.

STATEMENT	KNOW-PHRASE
Refining lignin from tree bark scraps can more than quadruple the vanilla supply within 10 years.	Let's get scrappy Scraps are delicious
By creating a "Man of the Year" campaign for the most stylish man in China, we can become top of mind for high-end fashion.	Fashion Means Man H&Man
By creating donuts inspired by chocolate bars, Dunkin Donuts can increase its revenue by 10% over the next five years.	The Nestle of Donuts The Frappuccino of baked good

Here is another great example. It's a commercial for Amazon. Notice they give you all the information, then sum it up with the Know-Phrase.

You can view all of these examples via the QR code or by going to publicspeakinglab.com/know.

DO YOU KNOW HOW TO BOX?

You might be experiencing a touch of analysis paralysis by now. With so many options, the question becomes: which one should you choose? The best way to think about it is that it's like boxing.

In boxing, you learn the fundamental trio of punches: jab, cross, and hook—a combination commonly referred to as the "1-2-3." Yet, must you strictly adhere to this combo? Not at all. You can use those three punches in any way you want: 3-2-1, 2-2-1, 1-2-1. Sometimes, you can craft both a visceral statement and a goal opportunity question; at other times, a Know-Phrase might suffice with a GOS.

The best way to start though is by just choosing one and using it as much as you can. Think about it like perfecting the jab until it's a reflex. Select one strategy above and consistently utilize it across multiple presentations. Practice it until it becomes effortless and second nature. For instance, I first honed my skill with just visceral statements through continuous use, much like certain boxers who build their entire careers around a single powerful punch.

Whether you use one of the strategies above or try to use them all, what's much more important is repetition. You need to reinforce your key message throughout your presentation, not just at the beginning. Think about it like an echo that resonates throughout your presentation. It's your theme, or in other words, the moral of the story, the one thing that I will remember and repeat to everyone else who asks me about the presentation (did you see what I did there, by the way?).

We'll talk about this more in the structure section but let me give you a bit of a preview. There are two ways that you can use repetition. The first and easiest way is to pick one of the strategies above and use it either at the beginning or the end of every section of your presentation.

Another method, which is more labor-intensive yet potentially more impactful, involves crafting all four summary statements and peppering them throughout your presentation. This strategy ensures you cover all bases, allowing for varied audience preferences. For instance, while one individual might resonate strongly with a GOS because of its concrete and measurable nature, another might be drawn to a Know-Phrase for its evocative imagery, catering to different audience inclinations.

This is probably most effectively used in callbacks in standup comedy. This is when comedians refer back to a previous punchline or expression during a routine. This acts to not only remind the audience of something they've already heard but also, perhaps more powerfully, to make the audience members feel like they are all in on an inside joke, making their routine personal and memorable. By creating a summary statement that easily links to a value judgment, an impression, a fact, or a course of action in the listener's mind and then referring back to it—calling back to it—you are also doing this. Just like how, with the joke, the only people who will understand the callback are the ones who initially heard it, the only people who will understand your Know-Phrase are the ones who initially heard it. The moral of the story is that repetition in the form of a callback will help your audience to remember what you want them to. It will be the thing that they say to explain your talk to anyone who wasn't there.

Here are two great examples of callbacks in standup comedy. You can view them by scanning the QR link or by going to publicspeakinglab.com/callback.

WARNING EXPLICIT CONTENT

TIME FLIES WHEN YOU'RE HAVING FUN

There's one common situation where we can use a summary sentence: when you are running out of time. Often, toward the end of a meeting or day, as things tend to drag in the beginning, we find ourselves in a time crunch near the end. It's common to witness presenters rushing through their remaining material because there is not enough time, but once the audience senses this rush, they mentally check out, and your efforts go in vain.

Instead of speeding through, use the remaining time to reinforce your main points by reiterating your summary statement. Redirect your focus toward this concise recap rather than racing through the content. As you finish, invite your audience to connect with you for deeper discussions or by sharing your contact details. This is sometimes a gift in disguise, but it can create even greater curiosity and increase the chances of follow-up and retention.

Remember, audiences tend to retain only one key takeaway. A savvy speaker knows this and strategically reinforces their main idea. Therefore, with ample time, restate your summary sentence in whatever way you'd like, but if you're running out of time, well… restate your summary sentence in whatever way you'd like!!! Leave them with the idea you want them to remember and repeat to other people.

ORGANIZATION

Let's remember: the goal is to make your audience curious enough to want more information. The trap that most of us fall into is trying to present to our audience all the details and reasoning that might be in an essay, when really a speech should be a SUMMARY of an essay. Instead of providing a comprehensive account of the details, it should highlight the conclusions, interesting points, numbers, facts, and most important, suggested actions. In other words…your 2%!

There is no right format for a speech because there are just too many different circumstances when you might be speaking. Instead, let's focus on one key idea when structuring your speech: REPETITION. Repeat some aspect of your GOS, VS, and Know-Phrase in every section of your speech.

Now, dear reader, I understand that with all that being said, it is still useful to have some structure advice, so I have included two speech structures here for you. However, these are not the only ways to structure a talk, so feel free to change it up as much as you want, with one simple caveat… less is more! Remember the 2%. A good speech is not about how much you give out, but how little. Make your listeners curious; motivate them to find out more on their own.

Informational Speech Structure

You can use the Informational Speech Structure when you want to EXPLAIN an idea.

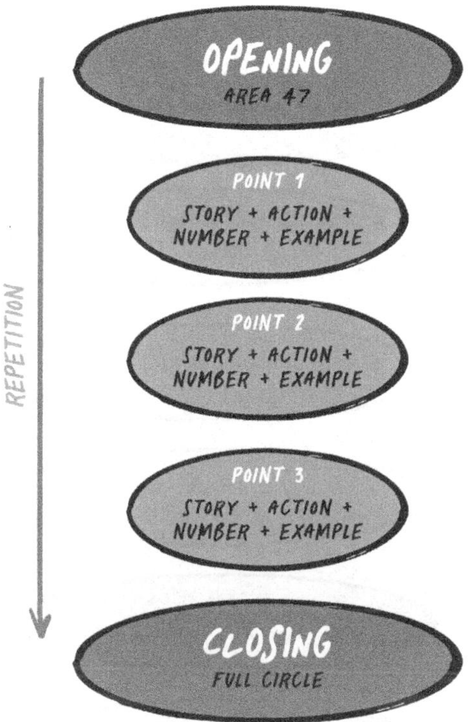

Opening should include GOS, VS, Know-Phrase, etc.

Each point should reflect back on the GOS and add some more information to it.

If people are only going to walk away with 2% of what you say, then the smart speaker takes as many opportunities as possible to repeat and stress their 2%. Notice the above diagram. At each point of transition or review during your speech, think about using your 2%. Add it to the beginning and end of your speech, as well, and you have a very high likelihood of audience retention.

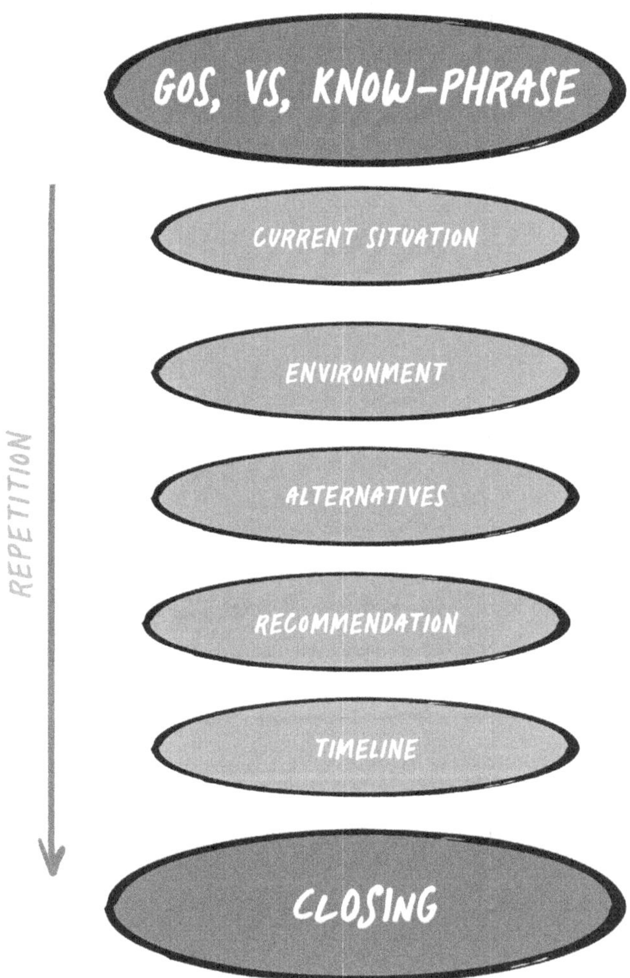

Case Speech Structure

The Case Speech Structure is best used to CONVINCE the listener of something.

Current Situation is anything internal to the company. It deals with financials, stats, key players, etc.

Environment refers to everything outside the company, organization, and industry. Think strategic analysis: SWOT, PORTER, PESTLE.

Alternatives are the most important part. Instead of trying to convince people by telling them what to do, highlight three different possibilities, each with a cost-benefit summary.

The ***Recommendation*** is one of the alternatives, the one with the most benefits versus the costs.

The ***Timeline*** is optional, but just make sure to define what is short-term and what is long-term.

Closing always recaps and refers back to the opening.
More on that below.

FACES, HEELS, AND THE THUG LIFE CAT

Have you ever watched professional wrestling? Let's talk about faces and heels. In the world of professional wrestling, "a face" or a "babyface" is a good guy and "to heel" is to be the bad guy. Now back in the early days of professional wrestling, promoters tried to create faces, good guys that the audience could support, but it never really seemed to work consistently.

Sometimes they would introduce a face, a good guy, and people would like them, but just as often people would boo them or not care. On the other hand, it was very easy to make the audience hate someone. In other words, it was very easy to make heels. What they figured out was that, when trying to get people to support someone or something, it is most effective to first introduce a bad guy. Then, whatever you bring in as the alternative is much more likely to be liked and supported. The moral of the story is: it is not easy to make people like something, but it is easy to make them dislike something. Or in other words:

 "IF A BABYFACE GARNERS NO REACTION, IT'S LIKELY THAT WRESTLER WILL TUMBLE DOWN THE CARD. IF INSTEAD THAT WRESTLER EARNS THE CROWD'S VENOM, GETTING BOOED EVERY NIGHT, WWE WILL OFTEN TAKE NOTE AND USE THAT TO ITS ADVANTAGE."

—RYAN DILBERT

You can see an excerpt of the article by scanning this QR code or by going to publicspeakinglab.com/persuasion.

Have you ever seen thug life cat? Let me make your day better. Scan the QR code or go to publicspeakinglab.com/thuglife.

We know from professional wrestling that it's hard to make someone like something but it's easy to make someone hate something, but what can we learn from the thug life cat? Well, it comes back to the concept of psychological reactance (PR) that was introduced earlier. It refers to the idea of doing the opposite of what someone tells you because you feel like your freedom to choose has been taken away. Here are some examples that illustrate this point.

You can either scan the QR code or go to publicspeakinglab.com/reactance.

It's a common reaction. Someone tells you what to do and you know it's the right thing to do, and perhaps it was the thing that you had already planned to do, but because they told you to do it, you wanted to resist by doing the opposite. That is psychological reactance. It's the need to resist when you feel that your freedom to choose is impinged upon.

So, what do Faces, Heels, and the Thug Life Cat have to do with organizing a good speech or talk? Before we answer that, here is another question: What is more important, the answer or how you got to it? It is almost impossible to get everyone in a group of people to agree on something, so finding the perfect solution isn't realistic. But if you can explain your thought process, show solutions that don't work, then present a solution that is much more likely to work, you increase the likelihood that people will choose your solution even if they don't agree with it.

Here is what you need to remember:

- Don't present just one solution. Present multiple solutions. This will help you to avoid psychological reactance because people will feel as if they have a choice.
- Make all your solutions, except the last one, into heels. When discussing each, present the pros and cons but stress the cons over the pros.

- Make your last solution the face. If you present multiple solutions, and none of them are ideal except the last one, that is the one most likely to be agreed upon by your audience.

OPENINGS

What makes a good opening? If you are like me, you've probably heard things like:

- A funny story
- An interesting statistic
- A dramatic quote

The problem is that it rarely works. You say your interesting statistic or your dramatic quote, and then what happens? Nothing. People just sit there with the "okay, so…" look on their faces. Also, how easy is it to be funny when you are nervous? Exactly! How does any of that apply to the majority of the time we are speaking? What dramatic quote can you apply to a quarterly sales report? This is advice for motivational speakers, and that is not us.

Now let me be clear, it's not that the above is wrong. These are technically good ways to begin a presentation, but they have one fatal flaw:

They require someone who is already charismatic/experienced to pull it off.

Therefore, what is the alternative? Before I answer that, let me ask you a few more questions:

- Do you like almonds?
- Have you ever tried cocaine?

You see, there's a part of your brain called Area 47, and in the book *The Organized Mind*, McGill neuroscientist Daniel Levitin talks about this part of your brain. If we were to peer into your brain where your temple is, we would find a region that looks like an almond sliver and is no bigger than your pinky finger. That is Area 47, and if we look at the research, Area 47 essentially does these two things:

- It tries to predict what is going to happen next
- It triggers dopamine release

Do you know what dopamine does? It is one of the feel-good neurotransmitters. Cocaine enhances the dopamine response. That's why it makes you feel so good…or so I have heard.

What does that have to do with how we structure our opening statements for speech? Well, again, if we look at the research, when you know exactly what's coming next (like in a standard presentation which repeats and elaborates on the slides that everyone can see for themselves), Area 47 does not need to predict anything, so it shuts down and you stop listening. When there are too many details, when you're not sure what the presentation is about and you're overloaded with information, Area 47 cannot predict, so again it shuts down, and you stop listening. But when you're sort of sure, when you think you know what the presentation is about but you're not 100% certain, or when you're actively thinking, "where are they going with this?" Area 47 is at its most active. Dopamine is triggered to keep you attentive and to help you try to figure out and predict what is coming next.

Knowing this, how can we activate Area 47? Believe it or not, quite easily, by asking a question or making a statement that at first seems unrelated to what you're about to talk about. Then, after a few sentences, the audience understands the relationship and there is an "Aha!" moment. I know this sounds strange, but let's look at some examples using the GOS, and you'll see where I'm going.

AREA 47 OPENING: Have you ever broken the law?

EXPLANATION (AHA MOMENT): When I was young, I once stole gum from a corner store. Of course I regret it, but what about people who don't regret it because they don't think that what they are doing is bad? That is essentially the battle we are having with graffiti. It doesn't matter how harsh the punishment is, it is always going to happen, so what if we didn't make it a crime?

GOS: By creating a graffiti safe space in the downtown core, we can decrease vandalism by 20% in one year.

AREA 47 OPENING: Does anyone here own silver?

EXPLANATION (AHA MOMENT): People buy precious metals like silver as an investment, but right now vanilla is more expensive per ounce than silver. In fact, most of the vanilla we consume is artificial because there is a global shortage.

GOS: Using lignin from tree pulp, we can more than quadruple the vanilla supply within 10 years.

AREA 47 OPENING   Have you ever done something you regret?

EXPLANATION (AHA MOMENT): Everyone put your hands up! I do something I regret almost every day when I am eating because I love donuts. I know they are bad for me, but I eat them anyway…and that is a good thing for Dunkin' Donuts, because everyone loves having a treat even if it's bad for them. The more interesting the treat, the more we want it.

GOS: By creating donuts inspired by chocolate bars, Dunkin' Donuts can increase its revenue by 10% over the next five years.

You can watch the examples by scanning the QR code or by going to publicspeakinglab.com/opening.

Notice something: there wasn't any question in the last video example from the show *Silicon Valley*. Activating Area 47 doesn't always mean using a rhetorical question or a show of hands question. Let's take our questions above and make them into statements.

HAVE YOU EVER BROKEN THE LAW?

When I was 15, I used to walk around with markers and tag walls. I had my own logo and everything. I never thought of it as a crime. I thought about it as something fun, and maybe one day I might become famous for what I drew.

DOES ANYONE HERE OWN SILVER?

I love baking, but I am super cheap. Every time I get excited to make muffins or something I instantly get discouraged when I see vanilla—it's as expensive as silver per ounce! What if we could produce vanilla from a cheap substance that we actually throw away? That is what I would like to talk about today.

HAVE YOU EVER DONE SOMETHING YOU REGRET?

I am addicted to chocolate. In fact, I eat it even when I am not hungry. It is my guilty pleasure, and that is how many people see donuts.

Can it be a picture? Yes! What would happen if, on the first slide, instead of having your topic and your name, you had something that created curiosity?

Imagine if before your traditional title slide, you did something like this (scan the QR code or head to publicspeakinglab.com/opening2.)

Think of these examples as a starting point. As long as you're starting off with uncertainty and then creating an "Aha!" moment, you will be activating Area 47.

CLOSINGS

Now that we understand how to open a presentation by using an Area 47 question or statement, the next question is, how do we close or finish our presentations? Certainly, we can review the main points and summarize our presentation using a GOS, but what is the very last thing you should say?

Make a reference to your opening at the end. If you used an Area 47 opener, all you have to do is refer back to it. In other words, you go full circle by making a reference to the beginning at the end. Let's once again go back to our previous examples and see how this works.

HAVE YOU EVER BROKEN THE LAW?

Let's not use the law to make kids criminals, let's use it to make them artists.

DOES ANYONE OWN SILVER?

The next big thing isn't precious metals or tech IPOs, it's vanilla.

HAVE YOU EVER DONE SOMETHING YOU REGRET?

Let's make regret something that people look forward to.

TRANSITIONS

Do you remember how we talked about repetition? How any good structure needs to be able to repeat the key idea over and over? How can you repeat yourself without sounding redundant? When should you repeat yourself, and how?

First, let's talk about the "when." The best times to reinforce your key ideas are:

- When you're transitioning between slides
- When you're transitioning between different sections of your presentation (i.e., background to alternatives)

- When you're transitioning between speakers
- When you're transitioning between ideas

The smart speaker takes as many opportunities as possible to reiterate their key message (using GOS, Know-Phrase, etc.). The best time to do this is when you are transitioning between your different speaking points. You may be worried that the repetition will make you sound redundant. That's possible, but only if you repeat yourself word-for-word. As you get better, you will find your own way, but for now, the statements listed below are all you need to make strong, reinforcing transitions.

NOW... LET'S...

- NOW that we've discussed point A, LET'S discuss point B.
- NOW that we have seen how to do it, LET'S discuss why we should.

NOW that we know that most health-conscious people still want guilty treats, **LET'S** talk about how we can position ourselves to be that treat.

NOW that we have seen how much market demand there is for vanilla, **LET'S** see what the potential cost is for this new process.

NOW... THE NEXT QUESTION IS...

- NOW that we know A, THE NEXT QUESTION is B.
- NOW that we know the problem, THE NEXT QUESTION is how to achieve the solution.

NOW that we understand that the value of a business is more than just the revenue, **THE NEXT QUESTION IS** what factors should we consider when making a bid to purchase?

NOW that we see that competing for the specialty coffee market is too costly, **THE NEXT QUESTION IS** should we try to compete with healthier donuts?

NOW that we understand that graffiti is a major attraction for tourists, **THE NEXT QUESTION IS**, is it right for our city?

The idea is that we can use our key message (GOS, Know-Phrase, etc.) as a transitional phrase as we move the audience's attention from one topic to another. We can reiterate our main message and introduce new concepts into the scope of the talk, effectively reinforcing our GOS and Know-Phrase as we delve further into new territory.

DON'T FORGET

- Good openings should engage Area 47 by using uncertainty to gain interest
- The best transitions use questions to reinforce the key message.
- A good closing statement should reference your opening.
- Any effective presentation should use a visceral statement or goal opportunity statement
- A slogan can be a memory cue to be repeated throughout your presentation to anchor people to an idea.

CASE STUDY

THE 2% IN A PINCH

Lisa is a nursing student who had to do a presentation about optimal patient care. She was the last presenter for the afternoon, and everyone before her had gone over their allotted time. Partway into her presentation, her instructor gave her the "two minutes left" sign.

"For a second, I totally panicked—I still had, like, five slides and ten more minutes to go. I thought, how the hell am I going to get through all of it, and then I realized that I didn't have to! I thought about the 2% (I used a GOS). I basically finished the current slide and went to my closing slide and just stressed my GOS for the remainder of the time. No one even really noticed that I ran out of time. They thought that was the way I wanted to do the presentation! The next week in class, everyone actually complimented me and jokingly repeated the 2%. The number of people that remembered, including my instructor, blew me away!"

CASE STUDY
REPETITION & RHETORICAL QUESTIONS

Daniel was giving a presentation for a student leadership conference. He had started a student-run social media group at his university, which paid for itself by contracting out its services internally to departments not fluent in social media. Daniel explains:

"I was basically trying to get everyone to try and do the same thing in his or her school. The idea was that students already have the skill set to do good social media just from their day-to-day lives, so why not use it to benefit other students and also to help the school? The students get something to put on their resume and a sort of job, and the school gets really cheap social media work that they don't have to hire from outside. So I just kept saying, 'You're already doing it for fun, so why not benefit from it?' It worked really well! I had all these people coming up to me afterward basically telling me that I convinced them to try it."

CHAPTER 3

LET'S GET PHYSICAL

IN THIS CHAPTER WE WILL FOCUS on your nonverbal communication. We will discuss simple strategies to communicate confidence even when you feel nervous.

PRESENCE IS MORE THAN JUST BEING THERE.

- Malcolm Forbes

THE BELLY BUTTON RULE

How much of communication is supposed to be nonverbal? Do a quick Google search and you'll see estimates of 60, 70, or even 90%. You've heard that a million times. What this means, for our purposes, is that public speaking is less about what you hear and more about what you see! Yet most of us focus on the things we are going to say and not what the audience is going to see.

You are the primary, and in some cases the only, visual that people will have. If you are not visually interesting, then your presentation or speech will also not be interesting. The value of information, its perceived validity and importance, is influenced by the physical communication of the person giving the information. Irrespective of the quality of his ideas, there are few people in this world that have more stage presence when speaking to an audience than Tony Robbins, so if you don't believe me, listen to him.

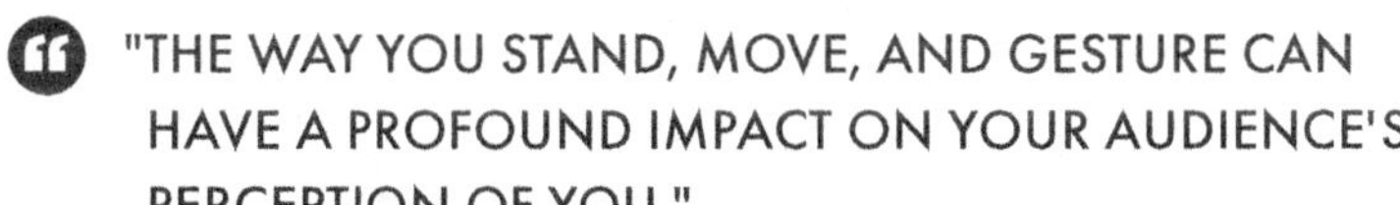

"THE WAY YOU STAND, MOVE, AND GESTURE CAN HAVE A PROFOUND IMPACT ON YOUR AUDIENCE'S PERCEPTION OF YOU."
—TONY ROBBINS

Remember the 2% rule. If listeners are only going to remember one thing you say and a general impression of you, then your nonverbal communication is the general impression!

Do you have a belly button? One of my big frustrations when I was trying to learn to become a better public speaker was asking trainers what you should do with your hands. They would always try to give some definitive rule or position that works, and it always seemed forced and fake. Quite honestly, whether it was with Toastmasters or with Dale Carnegie training, it always seemed like no one actually knew, so they just gave these generic answers. You hear all this stupid stuff like "never cross your arms" or "never put your hands in your pockets," but isn't that normal? Isn't that what we as normal human beings do when we communicate?

If you think about it, the best public speakers in the world are not politicians. They're late-night talk show hosts or they're stand-up comics, and they break all the rules about what "good" physicality should be and what "good" nonverbal communication should be. But who is easier to listen to, a corporate trainer or a stand-up comic? It's strange, isn't it? They cross their arms, they put their hands in their pockets, but they always look amazingly comfortable… why? Two reasons: they use the Belly Button Rule and they incorporate diversity.

Janine Driver is a well-known lie detection expert who works with the CIA and the FBI. She wrote a book called *You Can't Lie to Me*. In her book, she talks about the Belly Button Rule. She says that whenever someone is scared, or whenever they're nervous (e.g., when speaking in front of others or when lying), they will naturally cover up their most vulnerable parts: their groin, their neck and their belly button. Think about going into the fetal position. What are you doing? You're covering up your most vulnerable parts. From an evolutionary standpoint, you can think of it as protecting yourself from things that are dangerous or that scare you. Going back a hundred thousand years, it might have been a bear. Nowadays, it's a crowd of people.

Another way to think of it is the Naked Effect. When someone catches us naked, we instinctively cover up these same three points—tucking chin-to-chest to protect our necks and scrunching to shield our tummies as we hide our private parts—because we feel vulnerable. We can interpret the behavior as a fear response (for example, covering up our vital parts to protect ourselves from predators). The act of speaking in front of others also induces a fear response. It makes us feel vulnerable (under attack) and so we unconsciously—thanks to how the human species evolved—express that feeling through the same defensive body language.

This is one of those things that's hard to describe, so I've included it as a video you can scan or go to publicspeakinglab.com/bellybutton.

This goes hand in hand with other stereotypical defensive behaviors, such as rocking back and forth or angling one's body away from the audience. You will also see people "shielding" by crossing their arms (hugging themselves) or keeping their notes rigidly in front of their body. One, two, or all three of these body parts are always covered or shielded when we are nervous, unsure about what we are saying, or don't want to be in the situation that we're in. Think about your body position when you don't want to be in a conversation with someone—you angle away from the other person. Notice that these are all physical expressions; therefore, by stopping these physical actions, we can change the way that we are perceived irrespective of how we feel inside!

Knowing the Belly Button Rule is great, but how can we use it to our advantage? Again, I'm going to refer you to the videos to see exactly how this can be done, but let me describe it for you, because this is a physical tactic. I believe that being charismatic and being dynamic is a series of physical actions that you can practice, and here is how you start.

When you start to speak, put your hands in front of you like a robot and follow these two rules: First, don't let your hands touch each other, and second, don't let them touch any part of your body. That's it. It's that simple.

You can watch a demonstration of this by scanning the QR codes or by going to publicspeakinglab.com/bellybutton2.

If you start to use this physical tactic of not letting your hands touch each other or any part of your body, you'll notice that, periodically, as you get nervous, you're going to forget and start crossing your arms or putting your hands together… good! Do you know what makes stand-up comics or late-night talk show hosts look so natural and so confident? Diversity! I guarantee you that they're nervous, too; it's natural to be nervous. Yes, they use the Belly Button Rule, but they also have a diversity of gestures and movement. You see, the thing that makes you look nervous is not crossing your arms or rubbing your hands together, it's when you only do that. It's when you do your whole speech with your arms crossed or when you do your whole speech rubbing your hands together. But if you do it a little bit, it looks totally natural, because that's what we do when we're just hanging out, having a normal conversation with friends. Are you a people watcher? Stop and watch people the next time you are out. When we are relaxed and unselfconscious, we move every three to five seconds.

That is it, dear reader. The real secret to looking confident is diversity. Now that you know, go and watch some talk show hosts or stand-up comics, and you will see it too!

In summary, if you want to look confident, irrespective of how you feel, follow these three steps.

- Don't let your hands touch each other
- Don't let your hands touch any part of your body
- Occasionally break rules one & two

MOVING WITH PURPOSE

You almost never get to choose where you speak, but you can choose how you move within that space. It's all about how you use the space you have, the speaking area, to enhance the speech. When you are speaking, you can use movement and stillness to accentuate points and draw attention. Even in a small, cramped space, there is room for some movement. Do not be afraid to adjust furniture so that the audience is situated to suit your needs. If possible, before the talk, stand where you will be speaking. Take some time to see where you can move and adjust things, as permitted, to facilitate your movements. Martha Graham is a legend and revolutionary in the world of dance. Her techniques focused on physical movement (or lack thereof) to create emotional moments.

"THE BODY SAYS WHAT WORDS CANNOT. STILLNESS, WHEN DELIBERATE, CAN BE THE MOST POWERFUL STATEMENT A DANCER—OR SPEAKER—CAN MAKE."
—MARTHA GRAHAM

One of my big motivations for showing up early (an hour in advance, on average) is that it allows me to spend some time in the speaking area and to figure out where I can move and how.

When we are thinking about movement, everyone usually tells us what not to do, but I've rarely heard anyone talk about some practical strategies for what we should do. Before we get into that, though, I would be remiss if I didn't at least highlight some of the typical traps that people fall into, in terms of movement, when they are speaking.

Nervous energy has to go somewhere, and when we don't have a plan for how we can use that nervous energy, we will often start rocking back and forth on the spot or pacing endlessly, a few steps back and forth without a pause, in front of the projection screen.

That covers what you shouldn't do. Now that that is out of the way, let's talk about what you should do.

Finding Your Speaking Area

Frequently, when I am invited to run a workshop, people are filtering in or are already present while I am setting up. This facilitates the first strategy of becoming comfortable in your space. I use this time while I am setting up to start talking to people in different parts of the room. I make casual conversation as I move around my speaking area. By doing this, I identify where I can move to and still have a good command of the room. I then make a mental note to hit those spots during the speech.

You can see an example with the QR code or by going to publicspeakinglab.com/move.

This strategy provides two more added benefits. First, it breaks the ice with audience members, which will make the atmosphere more comfortable and help with audience participation when the speech begins. Second, it gets me talking and allows me to get rid of a lot of nervous energy. As you chat with people, you can give them little previews of what you are going to be talking about to make sure your words are clear and that you are ready to go.

You can take the time to ask about what they want to learn, and then tweak your presentation to make sure you address that topic. Don't forget to let them know that you will be addressing that topic, as it will build anticipation and interest. You can then use that information to encourage audience participation. Repeat the question to the audience or invite the person who asked it to share it with the group. Find out how many others were wondering the same thing. Doing so will add an interactive dimension to your presentation before it even begins!

What Is a Stage?

On the street, how do people know where to stand? Where does the audience end and the stage begin? The world of busking is fascinating. During the 2014 Buskerfest in Toronto, I interviewed several buskers about communication, and one fascinating finding was the idea of the stage. Unlike most venues on the street, the stage is not usually defined, and many buskers have developed novel ways to engage an audience. From magician Billy Kidd, mime Yosuke Ikeda, belly dancer Jaicyea, and many others — here are some of the interesting tactics they use to engage people, to make them take off their earbuds, to stop what they are doing and give them attention.

"You need to divide the crowd into sections. It is too easy to talk to just one part of the audience (usually like on stage), so I always imagine myself as the middle of a pie and I am always looking at different slices." *In other words, using visual sectors (which will be covered in-depth in the next section).*

"It's important that you do something that makes people stop and look, you know, something a bit out of the ordinary. Sometimes I do a fancy card shuffle to get people to slow down." *In other words, creating curiosity.*

"When there are, like, a few people who stop, you have to engage them fully. Don't talk over your shoulder or, like you know, tell other people to stop and join. You have to face them completely. Open up your body so they feel like all the attention is on them; you are giving them all your attention. If you are doing something in front of about ten people, other people will naturally want to see what's happening. It's FOMO (fear of missing out)." For me, this was a great example of using physicality to engage people. When you are fully facing a group and opening up (with your arms) you are showing confidence. *In other words, the Belly Button Rule.*

One last thing that I observed from a variety of buskers is the creation and then destruction of the stage. Many buskers would ask people to move in or out to create their performance space, but then instead of standing in the middle of the space, they would go right up to the audience. What did this do? Well… it forced that section of the audience to pay attention. It demanded attention! How can we do this? When you are creating your spots to stand, pick some extremes. Walk right up to people, to the edges of the stage. NO ONE DOES THIS when they are speaking, whether in boardrooms or auditoriums, so if you do, it creates the exact same impression that buskers create.

- It communicates confidence
- It makes the audience feel that you are really speaking to them
- It creates uncertainty and demands attention, because people never know where you will go next and so…they have to pay attention.

THE CLASSROOM

If you're giving a speech for school, it's probably going to be in a classroom, and it's probably the same one you have been in all semester. It will generally be easy for you to access the room.

A great strategy is to just stand at the front of the room a few minutes before class starts (not necessarily on your speech day) and start little conversations with participants as they come in from different parts of the speaking area. Be aware that in a classroom (as depicted in the diagram below), you will usually have at least five locations from which to speak (A, B, C, D, and E). By limiting yourself to location C, or the center of the speaking area, you will also limit your ability to engage the audience visually.

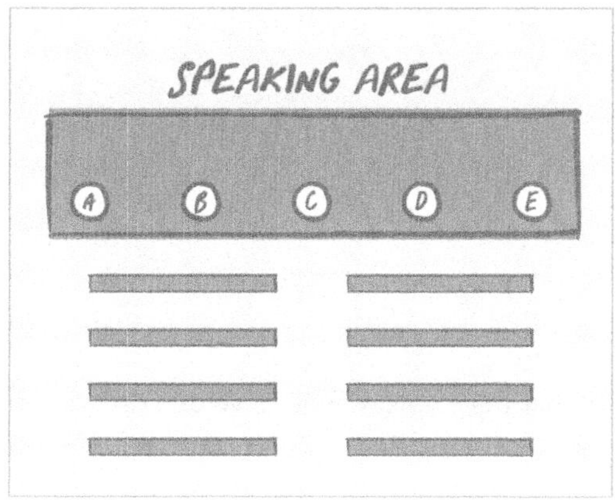

THE BOARDROOM

In the boardroom scenario, the room will likely be fixed and will be dominated by a large table. Once again, you can probably access the room either the day of or the day before you give your talk. Your speaking locations will generally be more limited than they are in the classroom or on a stage (as indicated by A, B, and C in the visual). I actually try to slide the table as far away from me as possible, so that I have more room to move around. If there is a chair immediately in front of the location in which you will be speaking, get it out of your way. I also adjust chairs so that they are facing me and not the table (or I ask everyone to do that before I start). Furthermore, I use this opportunity to explore the space and ascertain the best possible speaking locations for my purposes.

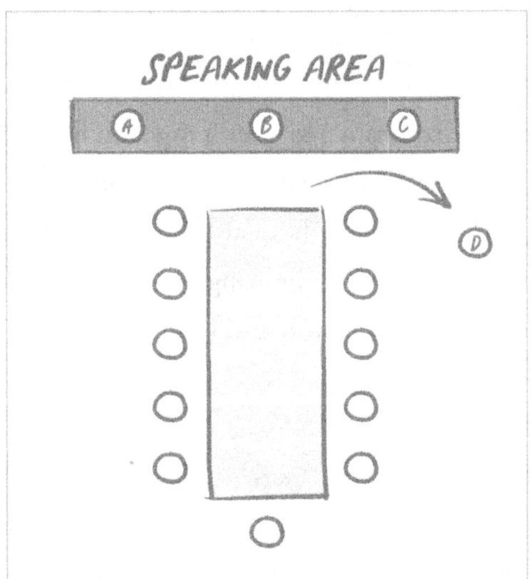

THE STAGE

Most stages, whether big or small, will have one of two general setups.

STAGE A

In the first, there will be a podium in a corner with the central area taken up by a screen. Alternatively, there will be a podium in the center of the stage or speaking area, possibly with a screen on either side of you. Like the classroom, you will likely have the full spectrum of locations from which to speak (A, B, C, D, and possibly E). The rule for either setup is: Do not get stuck behind the podium! In either of these setups, if you limit yourself to a single boring visual, people will spend more time staring blankly at you than listening to you.

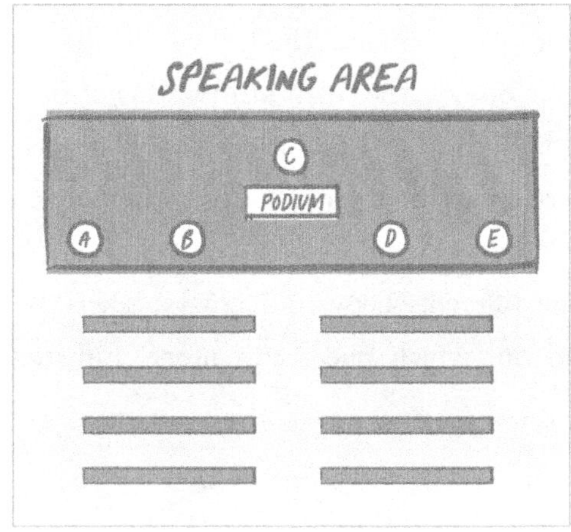

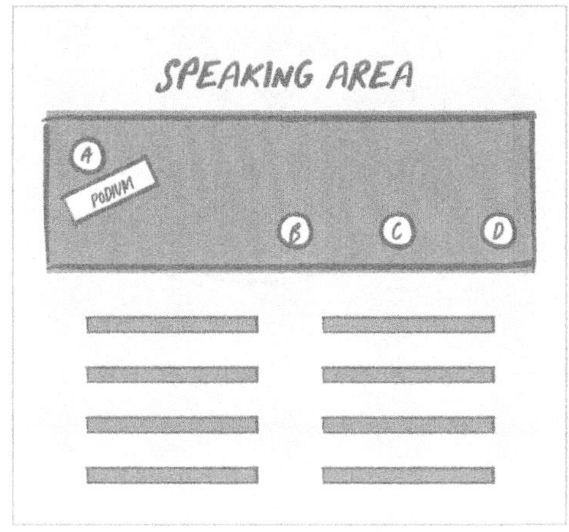

STAGE B

Now you know how to move. What happens when you can't move? What do you do when you are stuck behind a podium, and there is no choice? What do you do then?

Do you own a clock? Imagine a clock on the floor (see diagram).

When you are looking directly at the audience, it is 12 o'clock. In cramped situations where movement is difficult, you can angle your body to 10 and 11 o'clock on one side or 1 and 2 o'clock on the other side, to create the feeling of movement. The key to the angling approach is to rotate your whole body, rather than just twisting at the hip. You do this because of the Belly Button Rule. It gives the impression that you are speaking to everyone in the room. Let's compare two examples from the White House Correspondents' Dinner. Let's not think about politics, but rather, notice the difference between the two speakers. Both are great, but with the sound off, which one seems more animated, more visually interesting?

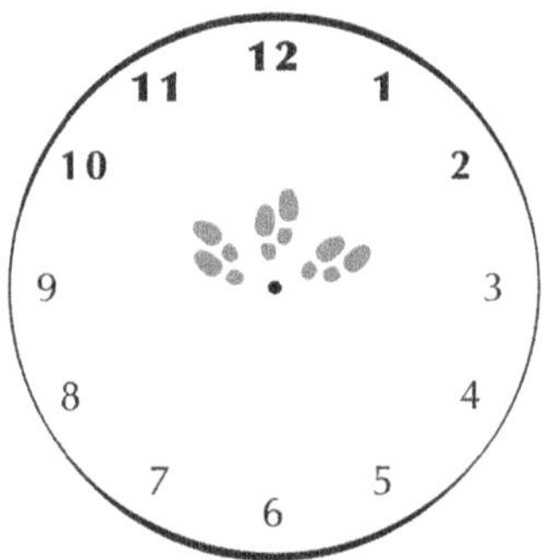

Scan the QR code to watch or go to
publicspeakinglab.com/clock.

Notice how Hassan is using his angles to really communicate to the whole room. This also gives him a much more dynamic and energetic look. This is how physical actions create a strong general impression.

In the 3rd video we see Opey Olagbaju again. I include this video so you can see that even without a podium you can use the clock strategy. Especially when you don't have a lot of room, as in this case.

EYES

The problem with eye contact is…is it a good thing or bad thing? Everyone tells us that eye contact is very important, and that you should always be making eye contact with people when you're speaking, and I agree. Sort of.

Eye contact is very important, but for what? Have you ever really thought about it? You're probably thinking that it is important to connect with someone, and that is the key idea that everyone brushes over. Connect with someone. You can connect with an individual, someone in close proximity, but what does that have to do with speaking to groups? Nothing! If you really think about it, the accepted belief that it's very important to make eye contact when presenting doesn't actually make sense outside of the context of trying to connect with one or two people in a specific moment.

Here's why it doesn't make sense. First of all, how are you supposed to make eye contact with 20, 30, 40, 100 people? How are you supposed to keep track of everyone you made eye contact with? What happens if you miss one person? Does that mean that person isn't going to remember anything? If I stop making eye contact with someone, do they stop listening? When we actually think about the logistics of eye contact, we start to realize that everything we have been told about it doesn't make sense when you are speaking to groups. Eye contact is for connecting with a person, not with people.

This is not just my opinion, either. It's rooted in biology. Your foveal vision is your direct line of sight. It is the only part of your visual field that has 100% acuity. Everything else is peripheral vision; you are aware of it but not processing it. Here is the problem. Your foveal vision really only operates within a short distance. Put out your arm and stick your thumb up. That is roughly the range of your foveal vision and anything outside of that is peripheral. To focus on anything in the peripheral range requires changing your foveal range and requires extra mental focus and resources. Just look at something that is more than a foot or two away and try to focus on it. How long does it take to start concentrating on keeping your focus there without zoning out? A few seconds, maybe?

This is important, because it is not practical to try to focus on things outside of your foveal range, and most of the time when you are speaking to a group (not one-on-one) everyone is outside of your foveal range! That means that you can't actually (physically) make eye contact with them! Have you ever noticed that when you are done speaking, it sort of seems like a blur? Musicians, actors, and speakers all say this. You can't actually remember much, and that is not just nerves. It's because most of the visual stimulus (the audience) is outside of foveal range.

Before we go any further, I want you to watch this video I made for you where I explain an aspect of eye contact that most of us haven't considered.

What happens when you are nervous while speaking and you make eye contact? You stumble or get distracted. And, of course, you will usually only notice the people who look least impressed, and then it's even more distracting because you focus on them. What about everyone else?

Why is eye contact so distracting? Because it is inherently a challenge. At its core, it means:

I fight you   I love you

Try this game: Find a friend and attempt to make direct eye contact while having a conversation. After a few moments, it becomes really difficult to have the conversation, and you'll realize you are focusing more on maintaining eye contact than anything else. You stop processing information, and it's hard to take in what the other person is saying because all your focus is on maintaining eye contact. How is that a good thing?

This is the problem with eye contact. It's not practical and it's distracting. Couple that with being nervous and you have a recipe that is guaranteed to make you stumble in your presentation.

If you want to do a deep dive into eye contact and how it tends to interrupt our cognitive process you can check out this QR code or go to publicspeakinglab.com/eyecontact2.

So now that we know the traps to eye contact and the problems with eye contact, the next big question is what can we do about it? If not eye contact, then what?

Rather than eye contact, what we should be striving for is eye and head movement. This will allow you to connect with the audience without getting distracted. It is easy to do even if you're nervous. Once again, it relates to the concept of patterns and change. What you need to do before the presentation starts (during the time when people are coming in or at some point before the session begins) is visually break the room up into sectors. The number and orientation of sectors and how they are placed depends on the room itself, and you can experiment with what works best.

In my experience, a grid pattern is most helpful. I have never needed to go beyond nine sectors. If the room is really big, instead of making more little sectors, increase the size of each sector. The rule is, the bigger the room, the bigger your head/eye movements need to be. So even in a large room, it's best to limit yourself to about nine sectors. Once you establish those sectors, all you have to do is try to move your head about every two seconds. By constantly moving your head and eyes, you will give the impression that you are talking to everyone in the room without necessarily making eye contact. As you get better with public speaking, you will find that you can make actual eye contact with more frequency. Even then, however, the use of sectors will ensure that you connect with the entire audience, rather than inadvertently focusing on one area or a few people.

CLASSROOM A

CLASSROOM B

AUDITORIUM A

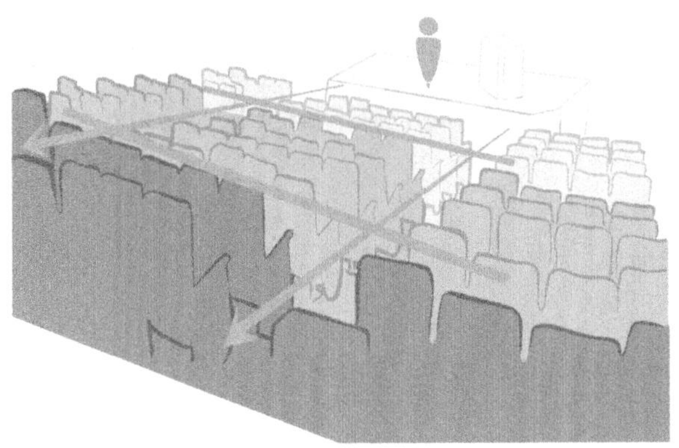

AUDITORIUM B

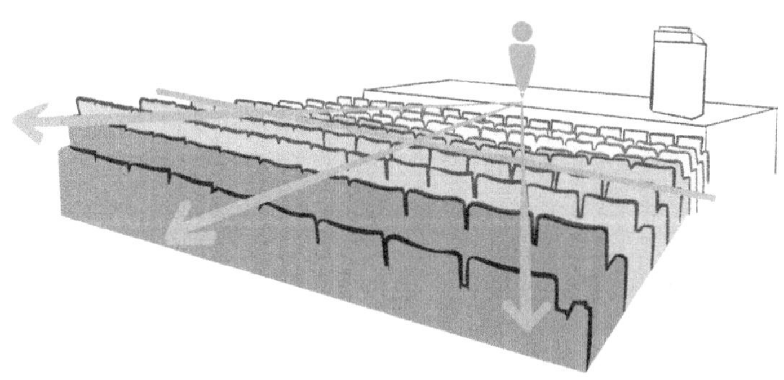

BOARDROOM A

BOARDROOM B

EXCLAMATION POINTS

How do you make something important when you're writing? If you were writing an essay, how would you communicate the importance of a specific sentence? Traditionally, it's by using an exclamation point. How can you communicate the importance of something when you are speaking? How can you make an exclamation point without syntax? Silence! In the words of the immortal Mark Twain, who was just as good a speaker as a writer,

> "THE RIGHT WORD MAY BE EFFECTIVE, BUT NO WORD WAS EVER AS EFFECTIVE AS A RIGHTLY TIMED PAUSE."
> —MARK TWAIN

Silence is powerful because it demands attention. If you've ever been in a meeting or a classroom and you're not paying attention, and you notice that the whole room goes silent, what do you do? Exactly! You look up suddenly. When someone is speaking, and they stop and the whole room goes quiet, you don't even want to move. Silence demands attention.

There is an obvious problem here, however. And if you have ever forgotten what you're about to say in the middle of a presentation, you know exactly what I'm talking about. That is an awkward silence, where even a few seconds feels like a lifetime, and all it does is make you look unprepared and weak. What's the discrepancy? What is the difference between that powerful exclamation point silence and that awkward, "I don't know what I'm doing," silence? Well, the good news is that you already know, because it is the physical gestures that you can practice. It's the Belly Button Rule. It's the visual sectors!

If we have silence, and we start to cover up our vulnerable parts or we start rocking and moving without purpose, then we look scared, stuck, and unprepared. If, however, we have silence and we stop on one of our points and Belly Button the whole room, it becomes a "mic drop" moment.

Once again, we've all heard that it's important to pause when you're speaking, but for how long and when? If you were going to write out your speech and you put an exclamation point at the end of a certain sentence, that translates into two to three seconds of silence. If you then combine that with using the clock idea to Belly Button the whole room during the silence, then your heart could be pumping, you could be sweating, you could be unbelievably nervous, but what the crowd will see is a confident and impactful speaker. (Insert three seconds of silence here!)

DON'T FORGET

- Practice looking confident by not letting your hands touch each other or any part of your body.
- Use visual sections to give the impression of speaking to the whole room.
- To stress that something is important, pause for two seconds.
- Use silence to focus people's attention before delivering an important message.
- Create two to four spots to speak from, spend some time at each spot you choose, and Belly Button the room at each spot.

CASE STUDY
USING SILENCE

Edward is an elementary school teacher. One of his major problems in class was drawing attention to what he was saying.

"I would think something was really interesting and when I turned around, I would see a room of glazed-over faces. It really started affecting my enthusiasm for the job. Also, a lot of the time most of the kids didn't even remember what I had just said. The first thing I fixed was how I started and ended writing on the board. Before starting to write, I would tell everyone, 'Look at this.' I'd then walk to the board, which took about two seconds, and in that time the room got so quiet it actually perked everyone up. I started playing around with this and would wait two to three seconds after I wrote something before I'd speak. It was kind of funny to see the students' reactions. Some of them would look up suddenly and others would stare at me and/or the board. It was really nice because when I chose to speak, I had so much more attention."

CASE STUDY

MOVING & USING YOUR SPEAKING AREA

Erin is a medical researcher and author.

"A few years ago, I was sitting in a giant auditorium listening as, one by one, the candidates for president of a society that I belong to gave their campaign speeches. Some of them were more confident speakers than others, but all of them stood behind the podium. That is, until the final candidate took the stage. She requested a mic so that she could walk around and address different areas of the room from multiple vantage points. Her talking points were similar to those of many of the other candidates, but she was easily the most engaging speaker. Guess who won?"

CASE STUDY
USING YOUR BODY INSTEAD OF WORDS

Nadia is a fitness instructor working on creating choreography and taking command of the class.

"So I had just gotten my certification and I was making choreography for a class. I asked Ivan to give me some feedback. What we noticed was that I was using lots of words to describe actions. In the heat of the moment, and with the music in the background, I would stumble over what I was saying, and I couldn't be heard. We worked on body language a lot. The first thing we did was role-play starting the class. He made me go through how I introduced myself and how I got everyone on the floor. We focused on just being still and open and on making people come to me, rather than me trying to go and collect everyone. It was really interesting to discover that if I walked out slowly and just stood in the front of the room, people would notice. He also made me use actions instead of words to get people to do what I wanted them to do. The more I did it, the easier it got, and it was awesome when I started getting compliments about my class and how engaging and confident I was!"

CASE STUDY
NERVOUS GESTURES

Nancy is pursuing a law degree. As part of her program, she had to participate in mock litigation to prepare her for actual courtroom trials.

"I was working with Ivan, and he recorded me doing my opening statements. When we watched the video afterward, I noticed that I kept clutching my left thumb with my right hand, and it made me look really uncomfortable. We worked on doing my opening statement without letting my hands touch. The first few times were really frustrating, because I just couldn't figure out what to do with my hands, and I kept fudging my words. After about the fourth time, however, I noticed that my hands and arms were sort of moving more naturally in the video playback. I was actually surprised, because I was still feeling nervous, but not having the obvious nervous 'tells' masked the anxiety I felt."

CHAPTER 4

BUILDING CALLUSES

IN THIS CHAPTER WE WILL ADDRESS fear—the fear of public speaking and the nerves that make you forget. We will face some hard truths and give you tactics to help you address them.

THE GREATEST MISTAKE
YOU CAN MAKE IN LIFE IS TO
BE CONTINUALLY FEARING
YOU WILL MAKE ONE.

- Elbert Hubbard

OVERCOMING NERVES?

It's time for another reality check. All the advice that you've ever been given about how to overcome nerves is wrong. Whoever gave it to you meant well, but they didn't know what they were talking about.

In fact, being nervous is a reasonable response to being in a stressful situation. Unless you can get out of the stressful situation, you will feel nervous and will have to somehow deal with it.

There is no such thing as overcoming nervousness because nerves are a physiological response to stress. Every piece of advice you've been given on this doesn't work. They say, "take deep breaths," and so you take deep breaths, and guess what? You're still nervous. They say, "do a bunch of jumping jacks or some weird physical action to release your nervousness," but you do that, and guess what? You're still going to be nervous. None of that stuff works. Sometimes people are advised to visualize the audience in their underwear or visualize them naked, but how hard is it to visualize when you're standing in front of that audience trying to remember what to say? It's not possible and it's not something you can practice. It seems to make sense on the surface until you really think about it or try to do it yourself. (On a side note, if you are intimidated by suits, shouldn't you picture the audience wearing Hawaiian shirts and flip flops or picture that they are adorable puppies with bows in their hair or something like that? Addressing a room full of naked people would be pretty freaky.)

The goal is not overcoming nervousness, because that's impossible. Instead, the goal is becoming so used to being nervous that it no longer affects your delivery. In other words, the goal is to build calluses to nervousness. How do you build calluses? It's in the way you practice.

How to Practice

Here is how most people practice:

- In front of the mirror
- Mumbling to yourself on the bus
- Mumbling to yourself in the car
- Mumbling to yourself walking down the street
- Practicing only inside your head, so no one can hear you
- Looking at your slides & mentally noting the things you want to say
- Reading your slides and then pretending to present

But then what happens when you have to present for real? You probably forget the first thing that you wanted to say and then you stumble or stutter because of the nervousness. Your presentation kind of goes off the rails. That means that all the ways we have been told to practice don't work. The reason that they don't work is because we have never practiced with the stress of being watched. That, dear reader, is the secret.

The only way to practice effectively is with the stress of being watched. That is how you build calluses. That is how you ensure that even though you feel the nervousness, it will not affect your delivery! Here are four strategies for how to practice.

STRATEGY 1 - IN FRONT OF SOMEONE

Find a friend or significant other and ask them if you can run a portion of your speech by them. They have to say yes. Sometimes that yes going to be very reluctant because they won't want to do it. This will make your practice even more effective because you'll be even more nervous.

Do this two or three times in front of that same person and you'll stop feeling nervous. Then, go find someone else. Do this three or four times and you will have built the calluses. When you have to present for real, you will still be nervous, but you'll be used to the nervousness, and it's much less likely that it will affect your delivery. In other words, it's much less likely that you'll stumble or forget what you wanted to say.

STRATEGY 2 - BY DISTRACTING YOURSELF

This is a practice technique that will allow the speaker to get accustomed to speaking in the face of distraction.

Practice your speech while doing another activity. By practicing your speech with distractions, you are solidifying the information in your brain and making its recall almost automatic. I like to practice while I am washing dishes, driving, shopping, or getting dressed. If you recite your speech while doing another action, you'll have confidence knowing that you can perform well even when faced with unexpected distractions.

STRATEGY 3 - WHERE PEOPLE CAN SEE YOU

This is the most effective—yet most difficult—way to build the calluses. Go to a park or a street where there are lots of people walking by. You don't have to engage anyone. All you have to do is practice your speech aloud, so someone who is walking by will hear you. Just whispering doesn't count. That's it. It's that easy or hard, depending on how even the idea of it makes you feel. Now you don't have to always go to extremes. Sometimes you can practice in the lunchroom when there are people around, sometimes you can practice in the lobby as you wait for the elevator. The main thing is that it has to be in a place where people walk by and where they can see you talking. And, again, it needs to be OUT

LOUD. Just so you know, by doing these strategies you are following in the foot steps of comic royalty.

I was working with the VP of a finance company preparing for a speech he had to give at a sales conference. After a few weeks, he was getting really good at delivering numbers in an impactful way, commanding the audience and all kinds of stuff. This VP was doing a great job. Then I took him out to a major intersection with lots of street traffic and people walking by. Believe me when I tell you, I took five or six steps away and said, "Now deliver your speech," and there were people walking in between us, behind us, and in front of us, and he couldn't do it. He got so nervous and so shy that he forgot how to start and forgot what he wanted to say. At least at first…because I wouldn't let him off the hook. It took about three or four minutes before he could say it out loud, so that I could hear, and he stumbled the whole way through. Remember that this was a speech he had been working on for weeks, and he had it down pat, but the fear of being watched completely hindered him. That being said, after about 20 minutes of trying, he was saying it louder. We did that three or four times, and by the last time, he was speaking loud enough that I could hear him from 20 feet away, and his hands were big. There were still people walking by, but he didn't care, because he had built up calluses to it. He told me afterward that the stress and nervousness he felt at the actual sales conference was less than at our practices and, as a result, he killed it.

STAND-UP COMICS AREN'T FUNNY

I remember the first time I saw stand-up comedy. I was a little kid and it was Eddie Murphy Raw. Wow, I remember laughing so hard that I peed a little (yup I am admitting it). Since then, I have been fascinated with the world of stand-up comedy, not just as a fan but also as a student of public speaking. Have you ever thought about how jokes work?

Every comic has "bits" which are sections of content they create. For example, you might have a five-minute bit about using Tinder or washing dishes. That means five minutes of comedy on that subject. A stand-up routine is made up of several bits, but how are those bits created? Are they written down?

For this book, I spoke with several comedians. One of the fascinating insights I got from those interviews was on preparation. There is actually a process that many comics follow to develop jokes and bits. They will start with an idea, maybe a few words that encompass the whole bit (almost like a VS or GOS!!), and then they will try to sneak that idea into their social conversation until they have a delivery that seems natural. Finally, they will go to open mic nights or comedy nights that are typically slow (small audiences) and try out their bits. This is essentially practicing where people can see you. Usually they "bomb" or fail and are not very funny at first, but by only practicing in front of crowds they are practicing with stress to build a callus to the nervousness and also finding their optimal delivery. Louis C.K. is a controversial figure, but his ability to look natural and conversational on stage cannot be denied. He said it best:

> "I GO ON STAGE AND I'M AFRAID, BUT THAT FEAR PUSHES ME TO PREPARE HARDER. JOKES DON'T JUST HAPPEN— THEY'RE CHISELED OUT OF RAW FEAR, POLISHED WITH SWEAT, AND DELIVERED WITH CONFIDENCE."
> —LOUIS C.K.

What we end up seeing is the illusion of "off-the-cuff," the illusion of spontaneity, because the final version of the bit has come from months of practice in front of others.

A NOTE ON NOTES

There are a couple of ways that we use notes. Normally, what most of us will do is to write our speech out word for word to make sure that we have everything covered in the right way. Then, we'll try to memorize what we just wrote out and repeat it perfectly. But you can always tell when someone has memorized something because the way we write is not the way we speak. In a perfect world, you would never need notes and you would never forget what you are about to say, but the reality is that it happens all the time, so notes become our security blanket.

Another problem with writing your speech out word for word is that, if you lose your place, it's very difficult to return to where you left off. Couple that with the awkward silence while you're trying to skim through your speech to find out where you left off. Two seconds of that feels like an eternity and you'll most likely give up and wing it anyway.

Sometimes, we don't even look at our notes. We just bring them up and hold them out in front of us. In other words, we use our notes to block our vulnerable areas and show everyone that we're nervous. In my experience, even speakers who have prepared well and know the key information to be communicated carry notes simply because of nervousness. The notes are meant to be a safety net, but they become more of a crutch. The speaker knows what to say but looks at their notes anyway to confirm. They do this simply because the notes are there. How can we remove this crutch?

Some of you may be reading this and thinking, "I don't write out my whole speech," but chances are you are writing out your notes in a normal size font and/or your bullets are sentences. If you do this, the same applies because it's hard to find where you left off when you need to be able to read through full sentences to do so. That takes a long time, especially when you're nervous and people are watching you.

There's a better way to both write and use notes. The note strategy I'm about to give you really only works if you use the practice strategies above. The good news is, if you couple these two things, they will 100% work!

Here's the big rule: Notes should not tell you what to say, they should remind you what to say. Think about it like the table of contents of a book. If you've read the book, you can look at the table of contents and it reminds you of what was in a given chapter. That's how this works. Here are three basic rules for how you should design your notes:

- Larger font
- One to two words per bullet
- One piece of paper

Let's look at an example below of notes for a presentation on why computers should be banned from classrooms. I used an 8.5 x 11-inch piece of paper and I filled it up. This was for a Toastmasters meeting from a few years ago.

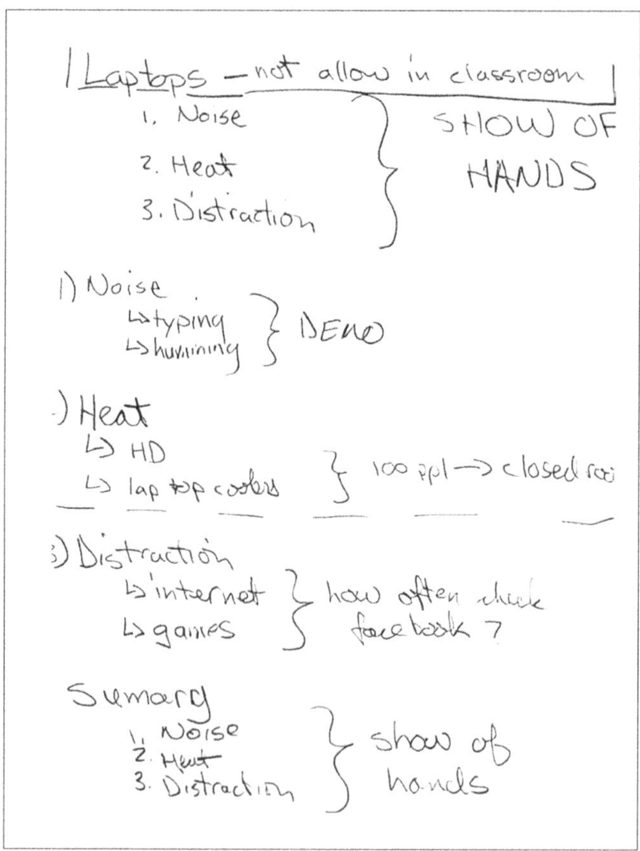

When you read the notes below, can you tell immediately what the presentation is about? Can you identify the main points and examples? If so, then theoretically, could you not give the presentation yourself right now using these notes? These are the criteria for effective notes. Without a solid yes to each of these questions, your notes – and thus your information – are not clear enough.

I suggest using a large font so that you can put your notes down on the table in front of you and still be able to read them from far away. Think 30-point fonts. As stated above, keeping notes in your hand is just a crutch and, even if you don't need them, you're going to look at them. It's always a good idea to put your notes down somewhere in front of you with large fonts that you can quickly read. We're talking…glance, got it, keep talking.

From the example on the next page, you can also see that by using just one or two words to remind me what to say, I was able to very quickly find out what the next thing to talk about was without having to read through things.

The UFC is the pinnacle of combat sports. Since nearly the very beginning, Bruce Buffer has been the ring announcer, and he has become an integral part of their live shows. With tens of thousands in attendance and millions watching on pay-per-view, how much stress do you think he must feel when he has to introduce fighters? That is real public speaking. Does he memorize everyone's names and stats in advance? No. That's impossible—or at the very least, it's really, really hard—so he uses notes.

Below is an example.

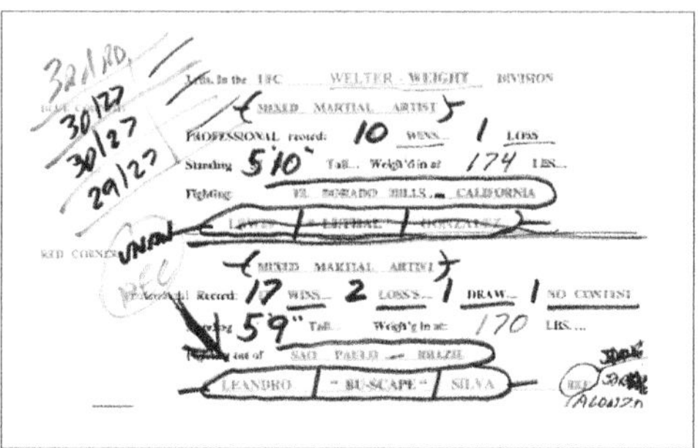

The first thing to notice is that there are no sentences here, and all the writing is very large so it's easy to see at a glance. The idea is being able to quickly look down and then look back up at the audience without having to stop and read. The most famous ring announcer in the world uses the note strategy that I'm advocating for in this book!

Let's go back to the world of stand-up for a minute. You may recall I mentioned that when a comic gets an idea for a joke or bit, they will usually try to write it down in a few words that encompass that idea. This is essentially giving themselves a reminder of what to say, not exactly what they should say. In the initial attempts at performing the bits, it is common to come on stage with notes, and guess what's typically on those notes? Of course, this is not a rule, but having seen a lot of comics and chatted with them after sets, I can tell you that the more polished the joke, the fewer words on the page. This concept is really summed up very well by comedian Graham Clark from Vancouver, Canada.

> **"I DON'T REALLY WANT WHAT I HAVE TO SAY TO COME OUT EXACTLY THE SAME EVERY TIME. WHEN I AM TRYING TO PERFECT A BIT, I REALLY JUST WRITE DOWN A FEW KEY IDEAS THAT HELP ME GET FROM THE BEGINNING TO THE END."**
> —GRAHAM CLARK

DON'T FORGET

- You can never overcome nerves; instead, build calluses to them
- The only way to practice is with the stress of being watched
- Notes are reminders
- Whatever you keep forgetting is the only thing you need to write down

CASE STUDY
SNEAKY PRACTICE

Mary is an account executive in a major accounting firm who rarely has time to practice her speeches:

"Basically, I work more than I sleep. Quite often, I am awake at 4 a.m. and work from home until 7 or 8 a.m. Then, I'm off to work 'till usually 9 p.m. or so. I am constantly doing presentations to clients, and often I am creating these presentations just hours before. Whenever someone at work asks me how it's going, or what I am doing, I respond by saying, 'Oh, I am working on this presentation for [client name]. They have…,' and then I get into whatever slide I am working on or the subject of the presentation. After that, most people (especially at the office) will engage me in a brief conversation about what I just said (everyone has an opinion). What follows is a conversation about the speech topic. I get to clarify what I want to say and practice what I want to say and how I want to say it. I get to test if what I am saying is clear and/or relevant. It's great, actually, because I never know when I am going to be engaged in a brief chat, and it always makes me a little anxious. But after doing this a few times, the words just flow. Even when my slides are not up to par, my speech always comes across pretty naturally. I once did this to a taxi driver on the way to a client meeting. I just chatted him up about tax reporting rules. As a side note, as I do my sneaky practice, I also refine my slides to fit what I am saying, rather than the other way around. Sometimes this is even done in the taxi on the way to see a client!"

CHAPTER 5

VIRTUAL AWESOME

IN THIS CHAPTER WE WILL TEACH you how to become more engaging online. We will also show you simple tactics to keep your audience interested.

"

VIRTUAL LEARNING IS MORE THAN
JUST A TEMPORARY SOLUTION;
IT'S A GLIMPSE INTO THE FUTURE
OF EDUCATION. IT'S ABOUT
EMBRACING TECHNOLOGY TO
CREATE IMMERSIVE, INTERACTIVE
LEARNING EXPERIENCES.

- Mark Rober

Why does performance in the education system, whether high school or university, rarely correlate with success in life? Someone who does really well in school doesn't necessarily do really well in their career. Someone who barely gets through high school may become amazingly successful. Why?

The traditional system of teaching is actually skewed. It's biased toward people who are good at memorization and regurgitation of that memorized information. That's what most classes test, but it does not reflect the real world. In what other part of your life are you required to memorize three months' worth of information and regurgitate it in one sitting? Most of us, when we need specific information, just look it up. It's our ability to apply that information that makes us successful. The fatal flaw in our traditional approach is that we've been teaching people to remember and repeat the material and not teaching them to apply it. The move toward live online learning is making this problem even more obvious.

I said this at the beginning of this book, but it's an important concept that you really need to understand. People say the future of education is going to be online, but that's not actually true. Online classes have been available for about 20 years. So, education is already online. **The future of virtual education is live online.**

Think about all the classes you have ever taken. On a scale from one to 10, how energizing, engaging, and interesting were they on average? I'm talking about high school and university courses and, if you can remember them, your elementary school classes. Chances are, with a few exceptions, most of them were probably pretty boring. And that's not the fault of the teacher, that's the fault of the process. Traditionally, the way we teach—whether it's in the business world or in school at almost all levels—is through lecture. It's someone verbally regurgitating a bunch of information that's probably already in the textbook that you have in front of you. How often have you been in any kind of meeting or class where you said to yourself, "I'll just get the slides later if it's important"?

People think that moving to online education or virtual education is more challenging, but I disagree. It's not that moving into online live lectures and meetings is showing us the weaknesses in our virtual communication, it's that it's showing us the weaknesses in our traditional communication. The boredom and disengagement we feel in an online class is the exact same boredom and disengagement we feel in an in-person class. The only difference is, online I don't have to be polite. Online, I can turn off my camera and just tune out and no one would ever know. If there's something that's important in what you're saying, I can always read the notes on my own time.

Although this chapter is titled "Virtual Awesome," the tactics that I'm about to show you can also be applied in person. You see, I believe that the way we traditionally have taught is flawed and it's always been flawed, but no one has given us an alternative…until now.

VIRTUAL YOU

Whenever I teach my classes on virtual communication, I like to ask participants how much of communication they think is nonverbal. The answers usually range from 50% to as high as 90%. While the exact percentage isn't crucial, the key takeaway is that a significant portion of communication is nonverbal. I think this is something we can all agree on.

This leads to the essential question: In a virtual meeting or presentation, how can we have nonverbal communication? Specifically, how can we come across as confident and engaging when speaking online?

During the COVID pandemic, I did extensive research on virtual communication while we were in isolation. I discovered that while many experts offer advice on this topic, not all of them practice what they preach. Instead of solely relying on traditional experts, I decided to study people who actually do it —those who speak to a camera, day in and day out, alone in their living rooms, offices, or bedrooms. Who are these magically engaging people? If you really think about it who is better at being interesting sitting alone in their bedroom then streamers and influencers? Whether for 1 minute, 10 minutes or even 1 hour. How are they able to keep viewers attention? Especially since most of them are essentially doing what we all want to do. Communicate information and/ or an idea to people watching us online.

I wanted to ensure my research wasn't biased by Western forms of communication, as many people ask whether these concepts apply outside of Western culture. I looked at YouTubers across the US, Latin America, Africa, China and India. While I acknowledge that I may have my own biases, I believe the principles of effective communication are universal. Certain fundamental aspects of how we communicate as human beings can be understood across cultures.

Here are just a few of the influencers I studied. I mainly focused on YouTube and Twitch because these most closely mimic a virtual meeting being long form, discussions and also horizontal camera angle:

Pokimane	Twitch	9.6 million
Miss Rage	Twitch	4.1 million
Bytarifa gaming	Twitch	2.1 million
CarryMinati	YouTube	31.1 million
HolaSoyGerman	YouTube	25.4 million
Yuya	YouTube	25.3 million
Marques Brownlee	YouTube	11.7 million
Philip DeFranco	YouTube	7.3 million
Nobru	YouTube	3.7 million
Nyma Tang	YouTube	3.3 million
ContraPoints	YouTube	2.1 million
Cecilia Cao	YouTube	1.7 million
Brian Jung	YouTube	1.3 million

I spent days watching videos and half the time not understanding the language and/or watching on silent to try to identify what these various streamers had in common. Slowly, I began identifying the characteristics of engaging speakers online. In fact, the more I watched (and it must have been over a 100 hours), the more I started narrowing them down until I finally identified two key characteristics that make influencers and streamers engaging—two characteristics that make them easy to watch, listen to, and engage with. Now of course there are many elements and the medium and topic have a lot of influence, but at a core level, at a human level, I found two tactics that we can easily use to become as influential as we'll...influencers. These two characteristics are: **framing** and **visual diversity.**

FRAMING

No matter the medium, all the influencers I studied consistently used what's called a mid-body shot—a frame that captures them from roughly the waist to just above the head. This frame is powerful because it allows a lot of nonverbal communication to come through. The speaker remains the focal point, but we also get to see their hands moving and subtle shifts in their body language. If you think about it, when watching someone speak on a stage, we naturally focus on them from the waist up. Mimicking this online makes a lot of sense. Remember, when considering visuals during a presentation, it's not just about the slides—it's about you. If you're not interesting to watch, your audience will find something else to look at.

How do you create this frame? It's easier to show than to explain, so I've included a few screenshots from influencers and an instructional video to help you get started.

Check out publicspeakinglab.com/frame or scan the QR code.

VISUAL DIVERSITY

How long is the average person's attention span? While studies suggest it can vary, it's generally shorter than in the past. If you look it up, you'll get answers ranging from 7 seconds to 30 seconds. If you're like me, you're probably thinking it's closer to 7 seconds—sometimes even less. Regardless of your opinion, this is a reality of how we consume information today. So, if you want to be more engaging, consider changing your visuals at a pace that aligns with people's attention spans.

Films, TV shows, and commercials change images roughly every 2-5 seconds, whether it's a different angle, a zoom, or a completely different shot. Most Instagram and TikTok videos also adhere to this.

But knowing this information, the question becomes: what do we do with it? It's one thing to know that changing visuals is important, but how do you do it when you're in an online meeting? Well, there are a few steps you can take. The first involves slide decks. If we are using them, we can practice sharing and not sharing them on Teams, Zoom, or whatever program you are using, in advance of the session. Many people start presentations by sharing their decks, reducing their camera feed to a tiny corner. This can be a missed opportunity for nonverbal communication.

Back in 2020, I remember running one of my first virtual sessions for a company on Teams. I wanted to try this strategy to keep people engaged, so I logged in early to the meeting, practicing sharing and not sharing my screen for about an hour to get it into my muscle memory. Do you know what happened afterward? During the last 10 minutes of the presentation, about seven or eight people asked me the same question in the chat: how did I manage to change the visuals so frequently? They found it really effective and engaging. You should have seen the look of disappointment on their faces when I told them there was no special button—it was literally just me manually sharing and not sharing my screen.

Ideally, we should try to alternate between sharing our slides and not sharing them throughout our presentations. As you get more comfortable, you can do this more frequently. The ideal ratio should be about 70/30—70% of the time, it's just you talking without slides, and 30% of the time, you're sharing your slides.

Now, you might be thinking, "Meetings and presentations are stressful enough, and now I have to think about sharing and not sharing my slides?" I know it can seem daunting, especially if you are not a technical person, but remember that this is a tool, and like all tools, the more you do it, the easier it gets. With that being said, here is a starting point... just do it once.

Here are two options:

1. Start your presentation without your slide deck—just you talking—and then, at some point, share your slides. I find doing my intro and then sharing either my agenda or executive summary slide as the first thing the most effective.

2. Start by sharing your slide deck, at the end of your first slide of substance (like the executive summary), stop sharing and talk about what it means.

What happens if you are not using a slide deck? Well, that's when we really rely on our framing to provide good visual diversity with our movement and hands. So, if it works for the biggest streamers and influencers in the world, and it works in local Teams meetings, isn't it something you should try?

Scan the QR code or go to
publicspeakinglab.com/visualdiversity
to see a few examples of changing the visual.

LECTURES IN ADVANCE

I remember watching a documentary once where they speculated about how many Einsteins we've lost to poverty or sexism, and I remember thinking how many we must've also lost to boredom. When I think back on how much of my life was spent sitting in classrooms just listening to someone reading notes, reading slides, or lecturing off the top of their head for hours, I want to scream. Lecturing as a way to communicate information just doesn't work for most people. If it did, we'd all be A+ students. Time spent together as a group should be used for group activities. You show me a class where everyone is sitting in silence for 80-90% of the time, staring, and I'll show you a class where no one is engaged.

Therefore, the first thing we need to do when we are planning for virtual engagement is to make all our lectures into videos that students must consume in advance. Then, the class time is spent coaching and:

- Reviewing that information
- Testing that information
- Applying that information

Now, you're probably thinking, "That doesn't apply to my situation." Let me answer that in two ways. First, this is just one tool of many that I will be introducing, and second, you're wrong and it does. The truth is, most classroom time and class planning is spent thinking about all of the information that needs to be covered, and we put very little thought into how to make our learners actually absorb that information.

Here's how to do it:

1. Divide your lecture into as many small pieces as possible with the goal of trying to make each section 10 minutes or less.
2. Use the screen capture feature in PowerPoint or Zoom (or similar) to record your lecture while going through your slides.
3. Provide your slide deck as an accompaniment to the video lectures.

I know this is easier said than done, so to help you on your journey, here are four different tutorial videos that show you how you can make your own screen-capture video lectures.

You can scan this QR code or go to publicspeakinglab.com/lecture.

Now that that part is done and all the traditional lecturing will be done in advance of the session, what are you supposed to do during your actual online session?

FOUR PRINCIPLES FOR VIRTUAL ENGAGEMENT

- Diversity
- Uncertainty
- Accountability
- Specificity

Diversity

When we interact with our learners, we need to make sure that it's in as many different ways as possible. By using a diversity of interaction, it becomes much easier to get everyone to pay attention. What do we mean by diversity of interactions?

Generally, we can divide how we interact with students in three ways:

1. Written
2. Audio
3. Video

Even within each one of these, we can have diversity. Suppose we are only comfortable using the chat. Why don't we use the chat to get a variety of responses in a variety of ways? For example:

- Yes / no responses
- Writing an example of something you just said
- Sharing a link as an example

The same thing applies when we have video enabled:

- We can ask our learners to give us silent video responses (for example, thumbs up, show of hands, or applause).
- We can ask them to speak to the group with video on.
- We can ask them to draw or write something and share it so that everyone can see.

The ways to interact are limited only by your imagination and by the requirements of your course. The aim of the game is interacting with students in as many different ways as possible and changing up the interactions throughout your seminar.

Now that we understand that we should be changing up the way we interact with our learners, and we have the technology, the next question is, how often should we interact with our learners? My general rule is for some form of interaction to occur every 30 seconds. However, I understand that you have to work on that, and at first it might be very difficult to arrange. So, I would recommend adding an interactive element roughly every 30 seconds to every five minutes. The good news is that the more you incorporate interaction with your learners, the easier it will become to do it.

This doesn't have to mean some kind of involved activity. It can be as simple as a show of hands on video or a "yes or no" response in the chat. Which brings us to the next rule…

Specificity

If we were in the classroom together, because of nonverbal cues, people would have a better understanding of how to respond or even whether to respond when asked a question. In the virtual environment we lose that, so we have to be very specific with what we ask for. Asking students, "What do you all think?" is not enough. Do you want audio responses, chat responses, a few words, or a paragraph? You need to be very specific. It's sort of like playing "Simon Says." Here are some examples:

In a moment, I would like everyone to write an example from their lives in one or two sentences.

Can everyone please type Y or N in the chat if you agree or disagree?

You have one minute to find me a YouTube video [for whatever task]. Please post the link, a start time, and one sentence about why you think it is a good example.

Accountability

If we are asking students to do things, then we have to hold them accountable and demand a response. To use one of the examples above, if we ask all the learners to give us a Y or N to show their understanding, then we must wait and insist on every student replying. If you have 20 students in the class, then literally say things like, "We have twenty students, but I only see five responses. Can everyone please reply Y or N?" Then you wait and, if you have to, repeat it again and wait. I cannot stress enough how important this is, especially in your first few sessions.

Unless you hold the students accountable, you have no way of knowing who is actually listening to you and who has just muted themselves and stopped listening. The good news is, as your classes progress, you will need to do this less and less as you will have established the expectations for response.

Uncertainty

This last one is the most important because it multiplies the effectiveness of the rest. If a learner never knows when they are going to be called upon or when they will have to interact and how, then it becomes very difficult to tune out. If you are just using the chat, but the students don't know whether they will be asked to write a letter or a smiley face or a sentence, then they have to pay attention. If they don't know whether you might randomly choose them to turn on their camera and answer a question or give an example of something, then they have to pay attention.

Now these concepts are great, but how and where can we apply them? Let's take these ideas and make them into practical examples that you can use. Let's pretend that you are running a training session of some kind. You have sent all the materials in advance as a screen recording of you reading your slides and expanding on them. You have let your students know that the expectation is that they watch, understand, and be ready to apply the information you sent in advance. Now what?

ICEBREAKERS

Icebreakers are important for a couple of reasons. First, they allow everyone to have fun and get to know each other. If we want people to interact, we have to first make everyone feel comfortable. Icebreakers also establish the rules of communication and interaction. If your icebreaker involves using the chat, then moving forward, you should have activities that use the chat. If your icebreaker involves people turning on their camera and microphone, you let them know that this will be required throughout the class. Let's cover three icebreakers that you can use in any situation.

Two Truths and a Lie

Likely you've heard or even played this game before, but virtually it takes on a different aspect. This is my go-to game to kick off a virtual session, especially when the group doesn't know each other very well, and it works in a couple of steps.

1. I demonstrate by getting the audience to guess my two truths and a lie. If it's a large group I'll use a poll; if it's a smaller group I'll use a show of hands.
2. Let everyone know that I'm going to put them into a breakout room and they're going to play the game with each other.
3. Finally, I say that when we come back, I'm going to pick a few random people to do it in front of everyone.
4. After we've completed the exercise, I let everyone know that the rest of the session is going to be interactive just like this game involving people talking to each other working in groups and demonstrating.

Complete the Sentence

This is a chat icebreaker that gets everyone using the chat, and we use accountability to make sure everyone participates. Again, this establishes the rules and expectations. Here are some examples.

- Look out, it's a ___________________
- The best breakfast is ___________________
- The only thing that scares me is ___________________

As everyone is answering, you respond and recognize answers. Once the game is done, you tell your participants that this is something they will be asked to do throughout the meeting: Everyone will have to reply and answer questions in the chat.

Video Scavenger Hunt

This is best for smaller groups where you can see everyone on one screen. Have everyone turn on their cameras but keep their microphones off. They all have to show something in front of the camera:

- A pencil
- An empty cup
- A piece of fruit
- Something with a company logo on it

You can recognize people as they complete the task to show them you are paying attention. Once the game is done, you tell your participants that this is something that they will be asked to do: They may be called upon to turn on their camera and demonstrate things.

Hybrid with Audio

I love bad, cheesy jokes. Get everyone to write their favorite bad, cheesy, clean jokes (in North America, we call these "Dad Jokes"). As people are writing, you can say the jokes or comment on them. Then you add an element of uncertainty by saying that you will ask a random person to turn on their microphone and say their joke out loud to the group. When you are done, tell your participants that this is something that they will be asked to do throughout the session: They may be called upon at any time and asked to turn on their microphone and speak to everyone.

If you want to see some video examples of icebreakers online scan the QR code or go to publicspeakinglab.com/icebreaker.

THE 30-SECOND RULE

Are attention spans getting longer or shorter? Your first thought was probably shorter! Young people on social media is an example, but it's not just younger people, it's everyone. It's you and me. In a virtual environment, it's even harder to keep people's attention. If they are on a laptop, there are other tabs and windows open. If they are on a phone, then they are jumping between your session and every other app they have. We have already touched upon this above, but let's go through a few more examples. Periodically (about every 30 seconds, if you can)

- get people to give you a thumbs up to make sure they understand, or
- get them to type something specific (for example, their favorite emoji, yes or no, etc.) in the chat.

It is also important to recognize answers, call out people's names, and thank them to show that you are paying attention and, of course, to hold them accountable.

PM CHALLENGES

This is another example of gamifying. If you give learners something to read in advance, you can establish accountability by asking them all to answer a question. But rather than answering in the group chat, get them to send a private message to you. Normally, when you ask participants to answer a question in the chat (for example, what are the characteristics of …? What was the example from the notes? What is the formula for…?), you will only get a few answers because there is no reason to answer when someone else already has. However, if we ask participants to answer via a private message, then they all have to do it, and no one knows who answered first. Again, you are using uncertainty and accountability to compel engagement. What if you have 100 people in your session? You don't have to check everyone's answers but rather just make sure that everyone provides an answer. If you have 100 students, you can keep waiting and telling them things like…

We have 100 students here, but I only see 20 answers so far. You have one more minute and I need to see an answer from everyone, please.

Come on, everyone, let's get those answers. I need to have a message from everyone.

Make sure you are not in the group chat, everyone, and let's get those answers to me directly.

As participants are sending you their answers, you can scan what is coming in and call out the responses you are getting, recognizing who is on the right track. There is an added effect here. For everyone who did not read/watch your lectures, you have established that it is important to do so. Also, the students who didn't do their homework are frantically reviewing your notes to find the answer, which means that they are learning!

BREAKOUT ROOMS

How do you create a lasting impression? How can you make an experience remembered and impactful? By making it a shared experience. In other words, by making it an experience with other people, and that can only really be done virtually through breakout rooms. A breakout room is a function that most virtual meeting and presentation services provide. It allows you to divide your participants or audience into smaller groups where they can have discussions and group work. I try to use breakout rooms as often as possible, in two- to five-minute increments, getting students to complete tasks in groups.

There are three elements that make breakout rooms effective. The first one we've already covered, and that is uncertainty. If they never know when you're doing breakouts, or who they're going to be in a breakout room with, that encourages engagement and makes it difficult to stop listening. Put yourself in the student's position. If you know that at some point, you're going to be put into a breakout room, where you will have to review something from the readings or discuss some part of the lectures, it's very motivating. You don't want to be the one person out of four who didn't do the assignment, for example. In the breakout room, it'll become very obvious, so therefore you are much more likely to do the assignment.

The next element is unrealistic time constraints. Giving students unrealistic time constraints, but actually allocating more time than promised, will help to hyper-focus learners and make them work as effectively as possible. For example, you could tell participants that they have five minutes to do a bunch of research, something that might normally take 15 minutes, but you actually give them 10 to 15 minutes to do it. Giving unrealistic time constraints, but then allocating more time, is just a great way to keep everyone engaged and hyper-focused.

The last element for an effective breakout room is a deliverable. At the end of the breakout room session, participants will have to present, post something in the chat, or send a private message. Yet again, I'm adding another layer of motivation. It's not enough to just get people to discuss something, because unless they have something to deliver afterward, there's no motivation. But if they know they're going to be called upon after the breakout room, then there is much more motivation.

Now that we know how to use breakout rooms, the next question is: What should we use breakout rooms for? Again, this is only limited by your imagination, but here are a few of my favorites:

- LEARNER BECOMES THE TEACHER. Put students into groups and make them each responsible for teaching the rest of the class some part of the module, topic, etc. You can be there to give them coaching or cover anything they might have missed afterward.
- LEARNERS MUST DECIDE. Give students three choices. Put them in the breakout room, and tell them that when they come back, you will select a random group to turn on their cameras and microphones and speak about which one they chose and why. Notice that I am again adding uncertainty, because if no one knows who will be called upon at the end of breakout room session, then everyone has to participate.
- SCAVENGER HUNTS. Learners need to find an example of something. It can be a photo, video, article, etc. When breakout room time is finished, you will call upon a random person or group to share what they found and why.

QUESTIONS AND FEEDBACK

Diversity is a beautiful thing, and what is more diverse than technology? "Backchanneling" is just a term that means using technology outside of your video conferencing interface. If you are using Zoom, Blackboard, GoToMeeting, Microsoft Teams, etc., it means going outside of those technologies to have other forms of interaction.

The next question is: What technologies and how can we use them? Let's take a look at two of my favorites.

Virtual Questions

People often ask questions in the chat during a webinar, but there's usually lots of people writing, so questions can get lost in the comments. You have to scroll to find them, and it's easy to miss things. What if we provided everyone with a link to a Google Doc where people could enter their questions? That would be much easier to manage and refer to. Also it would give us an easy to access record of all the questions asked without having to scroll through all the comments on a chat.

This strategy has a few advantages:

- It allows you to curate questions
- It allows participants to see questions at a glance (and can reduce repeat questions)
- It prevents the speaker from being distracted by questions
- It allows the speaker and/or host to review questions easily

Virtual Feedback

During a presentation, how can we keep other participants attentive when it's not their turn to speak? We need to have some way for people to comment and ask throughout. If we rely on the chat, however, the comments may be lost, and even worse, may distract the speaker and cause us to stop and go on tangents.

We need to have another platform where participants can ask questions. While the way you do this is limited only by your imagination, comfort, and time, as there are a ton of online resources, here are two that I find both easy and effective: Slido and Google Forms.

For both all you need is to provide a link, which allows everyone to provide their feedback, ideas, and questions for the speaker anonymously. But how do you make sure that everyone will actually do it since this will be anonymous? You can use accountability (for example, there are 20 students and you wait until you get 20 responses in the Google Form) or…

You can also use uncertainty. We do this by letting our participants know that everyone will be required to fill out the Google Form, but at the end of each presentation, you will pick a random student to give live feedback to the speaker.

It is easy to find to find tutorials on Slido, but I have made a video to outline how we can use a Google Form. Scan the code or head to publicspeakinglab.com/form.

DON'T FORGET

- Prerecord lectures and send them in advance.
- Maintain engagement with a diversity of interaction and activities.
- Hold everyone accountable, make sure everyone interacts.
- Be very specific with the type and method of feedback.
- Effective breakout rooms have a deliverable and uncertainty.

CASE STUDY
30 SECOND RULE

Javier works in sales in the automotive industry.

"As far as I have seen, no one from the automotive industry (in Mexico) uses their camera while doing video conferences. As you can imagine, this makes it even harder to connect with customers in virtual communication. We made a presentation tailored for a customer's specific needs and had some videos of examples showing what we have done in the past for other customers. During the conference call (unfortunately no one was using cameras) we were changing from showing slides, to showing videos, to stopping sharing and just focusing on an audio discussion. My colleague and I called it 'playing info volleyball' with the customer, since he says some things, then I complement with more info, then we go back to slides, then we show some videos, then back to the customer asking for more info (so we keep the ball moving)."

WORDS OF WISDOM

So what are you going to do now? Reading this book is the easy part; using it is another story altogether. This is what I want you to do the next time you have to give a speech:

- Do what you normally do
- Pick one tactic in this book
- Try it out in front of someone

If you do this, I can almost guarantee you that you will improve. Why? I once interviewed a very successful reporter. I asked them, "What do you think makes a story impactful or memorable?"

Here's what they told me. When they plan to present to the public, the first question they have to answer is, "What is the one thing we are going to say that the listener will repeat to everyone else?" If they can't find that nugget of truth, they don't do the story. At the end of the day, it's not about all the things that they are going to present, it's about the one thing their listener will remember and repeat to everyone else. From academia to debaters, to YouTube videos, to stand-up comics, this is the one thing that you need to remember. It's not what you say, but what the listener will retain.

Everything in this book has been focused on two central ideas that can be summed up in these two quotes:

> 99% OF THE POPULATION IS AFRAID OF PUBLIC SPEAKING, AND OF THE REMAINING 1%, 99% OF THEM HAVE NOTHING ORIGINAL AND INTERESTING TO SAY."
> — JAROD KINTZ

> "THE TWO WORDS 'INFORMATION' AND 'COMMUNICATION' ARE OFTEN USED INTERCHANGEABLY, BUT THEY SIGNIFY QUITE DIFFERENT THINGS. INFORMATION IS GIVING OUT; COMMUNICATION IS GETTING THROUGH."
> — SYDNEY J. HARRIS

Before reading this book, every time you had to plan a presentation or speak in front of others, what did you do? Did you prepare all the things you were going to say? Of course, but did you think about what the audience is going to actually remember? Did you think about what the audience will actually understand? Did you think about what the audience will repeat afterward if asked what the presentation was about?

Every time I use these tactics, I switch my focus from all the things I want to say to what my audience will actually remember, and now you can too.

NOTE FROM THE AUTHOR

I have always found writing to be very hard. My strength has always been in speaking, so I actually dictated this whole book. As I mentioned at the beginning, I wrote this book out of frustration, because after thousands of years of spoken language, the vast majority of us still fail at it. As I was dictating the book, I found myself raising my voice and getting really worked up because I care about this. I believe that being a dynamic speaker and commanding attention is a physical action that you can practice. I said it throughout this book and hopefully have proven that to you.

With all that being said, I know that I made a lot of very strong statements here about what is, and is not, good public speaking. But I don't just talk the talk. I will back it up. If you ever want to reach out with specific questions about public speaking, or challenges about how you can make a specific kind of speech interesting, then my doors are open. Challenge me. And I challenge you to be a better speaker than you are! I challenge you to take the ideas in the book and help me to #endboring.

YOU ARE NOW PART OF THE TEAM, SO LET'S CONNECT:

publicspeakinglab.com/contact

This is just the beginning of your journey. Join our community and get an 8-part "Ditch the Dull" Bootcamp that will give you even more tactics to overcome your nervousness and speak not just so people will listen, but so they will remember:
https://publicspeakinglab.com/join

If this book has helped you, think about what it could do for your team? Bulk orders are available at:
https://publicspeakinglab.com/bulk

Inspired by these ideas? Let's bring them to life. Book me as your next keynote speaker or workshop facilitator:
https://publicspeakinglab.com/contact

CONNECT WITH ME

THANK YOU FOR READING!

If you enjoyed **End Boring**, please leave a review on Goodreads or on the retailer site where you purchased this book.

Made in the USA
Monee, IL
14 April 2026

48327417R00083